THE STUDY OF
COMPARATIVE GOVERNMENT
AND POLITICS

THE STUDY
OF
COMPARATIVE
GOVERNMENT
AND
POLITICS

GUNNAR HECKSCHER
Professor of Political Science
in the University of Stockholm

WITH A PREFACE
BY
WILLIAM A. ROBSON

GREENWOOD PRESS, PUBLISHERS
WESTPORT, CONNECTICUT

The Library of Congress has catalogued this publication as follows:

Library of Congress Cataloging in Publication Data

Heckscher, Gunnar, 1909–
    The study of comparative government and politics.

    Report of a conference held by International
Political Science Association in Florence, April 5–10,
1954.
    Reprint of the ed. published by Allen & Unwin, London.
    1. Comparative government. I. International
Political Science Association. II. Title.
[JF128.H4 1973]   320.3   73–721
ISBN 0-8371-6789-2

$$JF$$
$$128$$
$$\cdot H4$$
$$C\ 2$$

Originally published in 1957 by George Allen & Unwin
Ltd., London

Reprinted with the permission of George Allen & Unwin, Ltd.

First Greenwood Reprinting 1973

Library of Congress Catalogue Card Number 73-721

ISBN 0-8371-6789-2

Printed in the United States of America

PREFACE

THE work by Professor Gunnar Heckscher which is now published for the first time is the report of a round table conference on teaching and research in comparative government held by the International Political Science Association in Florence from April 5–10, 1954. Although Professor Heckscher has drawn freely and fully on the papers contributed to the round table, and on the discussions which took place there, his essay is far more than a 'report' in the ordinary sense of the word. It is, I believe, the first monograph to explore at length the methodological problems involved in the study of comparative government and politics.

The subject was admirably suited to an international meeting of political scientists. For it bears on the question how far conclusions drawn from the experience of one country can be validly applied to the political systems of other countries; and the conditions which must be taken into account in attempting to answer that question. Can the data of government and politics be regarded as strictly comparable in any sense, or is it unique to the particular countries from which it is drawn? What are the merits and demerits of the different methods of approaching the subject? How far must the political scientist rely on the findings of neighbouring disciplines, such as history or economics or sociology, in studying a foreign country? What do we mean by area studies? These are a few of the significant points on which those who organised the meeting hoped an international discussion would throw some light.

My own interest in the subject had been stimulated by a report I had prepared for I.P.S.A. on *The University Teaching of Political Science* (published by UNESCO in 1954). This was based on national reports from twelve selected countries, in all of which some teaching of comparative government takes place. I was also aware of the intense interest in the methodology of comparative government and politics aroused by the challenging ideas put forward by a group of American political scientists at a seminar held in Evanston, Illinois, in 1952 and of which a report was published in the *American Political Science Review* in 1953.[1]

The round table in Florence was attended by about forty political scientists coming from twelve countries, including some situated in Western Europe, some in North and South America, and some in Asia. Thirty papers were contributed on different aspects of the subject: these papers were grouped round the following themes, to which separate discussion sessions were devoted:

> The nature, scope and purpose of the study of comparative government
> Studies of particular areas
> Democratic control of foreign policy
> Political parties
> Contemporary revolutionary movements
> Parliamentary procedure
> Electoral systems and elections
> Nationalised industries
> Methods of research and methods of teaching.

It was hoped to print some of these papers in the present volume, and this was the desire of Professor Heckscher; but it was unfortunately not possible for the publishers to do this from a commercial point of view.

It fell to me, as president of I.P.S.A. at the time, to appoint Professor Heckscher to act as the rapporteur-general of the

[1] 'Research in Comparative Politics.' Vol. XLVII, September 1953, p. 641.

round table meeting. The outstanding quality of his report shows that my decision was a fortunate one. I wish to thank Professor Heckscher warmly for his great efforts on behalf of the International Political Science Association. I hope that a wide circle of political scientists in many countries will recognise his report as a masterly presentation of the main problems of methodology involved in the study of comparative government and politics. It deserves to be regarded as an indispensable introduction to the subject which every student should read.

The discussions at Florence were of a most stimulating character and often reached a very high level. There was a great clatter of debate by the exponents of different schools and the proponents of diverse outlooks. Traditionalists and innovators were both well represented; and there were participants from some of the neglected countries as well as from the favoured lands which have been the happy hunting grounds of writers on comparative government. At the end of the meeting everyone had learnt something, and most of us felt our horizons had been broadened.

The International Political Science Association received a generous grant from the Ford Foundation which enabled it to invite certain eminent scholars from the United States who otherwise would not have been able to attend. The cordial thanks of I.P.S.A. have already been conveyed to the Ford Foundation. UNESCO has been closely associated with the present project from its beginning. As part of its activities in the field of teaching of political science, UNESCO has been a co-sponsor of the present study and has made a financial contribution to the holding of the meeting as well as to the preparation of the present report.

Florence was an ideal setting for the round table meeting, which was held there by invitation of the Italian Political and Social Sciences Association. The beauty of the city and its works of art; the loveliness of the surrounding countryside and neighbouring towns; the warmth and splendour of the hospitality which was offered to the members of the round table, contributed greatly both to the success of the meeting and to the enjoyment of those who attended it. To Professor F. Vito, President of the Italian Political and Social Sciences Association, and to Professor G. Maranini, President of the Faculty of Political Sciences in the University of Florence, our thanks are specially due.

WILLIAM A. ROBSON
London School of Economics
and Political Science
October, 1956

CONTENTS

PART ONE

INTRODUCTION

THE need of studying comparative government has always been recognised. In fact, all the classical works on political theory were more or less based on a comparative approach. It is known that Aristotle prepared a number of studies of various governments before embarking on his *Politics*; medieval authors, while less eclectic in their approach, yet attempted to bring in as much comparison as was possible under the circumstances; and in the seventeenth century comparisons of different types of government appeared practically in every page of political philosophy. One has only to glance through some chapters of, e.g., Montesquieu and Rousseau to note the enormous importance given by them to the findings of comparative government. When the study of political science was established in the nineteenth century, a number of the most important works were monographs dealing with only one country. Yet no one reading Bagehot or Dicey can fail to observe that some of their most important ideas are based on comparison; and there were in this period other authors consciously attempting a presentation in the field of comparative government, such as Ostrogorski and Bryce.

Recently, the method of comparison has come under intensified discussion. Indirectly, already some of the older works discuss questions of this type, but it is only in the last ten years that interest in methodological problems has become conscious. A report by a research panel in comparative government was published in 1944. The UNESCO handbook in *Contemporary Political Science* at least touched on the question. It was discussed to a considerable extent at the round table on the teaching of political science organised by I.P.S.A.

in 1952 and in the subsequent report by W. A. Robson.[1] The interest shown on this occasion was, in fact, the main reason for I.P.S.A.'s decision to devote a particular round table to the study of comparative government. In the meantime the report of the inter-university seminar organised at Evanston by the Social Science Research Council in the summer of 1952 had been published together with comments. Obviously, this report loomed rather large in the discussions at the international round table, although it was originally meant to be only tentative and explorative. As a means of stimulating discussion it was, however, extremely successful.

The international round table organised by I.P.S.A. was held in Florence April 5–10, 1954, under the very favourable auspices created by the Italian Political Science Association. It comprised over fifty participants drawn from fourteen different countries. Twenty-seven working papers, dealing with various aspects of the problem, were submitted by the participants.

In preparing the following report, the reporter has felt free to draw extensively on the papers and other contributions by the participants of the round table, even though it has not been possible to make explicit reference to them except in comparatively few cases. He is, therefore, particularly anxious to express already at the outset his feeling of gratitude towards all those who co-operated in achieving whatever results were gained at the Florence meeting. On the other hand, no formal agreement was reached or even attempted as to the conclusions, and on a considerable number of points major disagreements remained at the end of the discussions. The reporter, therefore, is responsible not only for the presentation of the subject matter but also for all conclusions and opinions presented in the report.

It is true that terms like 'comparative government' (or 'comparative politics')—as well as so many other descriptions of

[1] *The University Teaching of Political Science* published by UNESCO.

practical scientific fields—are *des étiquettes procédurales* and that no absolute or precise limits can be stated as to what should or should not be included in the study. This vagueness is at the back of certain difficulties which will appear in the following. At the same time, except for certain border-line cases there seems to be general agreement as to what is meant by the term. There is also agreement on the importance of studying it and on the whole even on the reasons for which such a study is regarded as profitable.

It is almost a platitude to point out what these reasons are. Comparative studies are the core of any study of 'foreign' governments. They are of pedagogical importance, especially if we are to gain a reasonably realistic and relativistic view of our own government. Because of the growth of international contacts, scientific, political or economic comparisons between different countries, as well as a knowledge of foreign institutions, are of great practical value.

These reasons may be called 'informational' or 'utilitarian.' They include the pragmatic approach: we want to draw on foreign examples which may give us ideas for the development of our own institutions. Similarly, we may flatter ourselves that a knowledge of our institutions may help others: 'the discipline has a mission to fulfil in imparting our experience to other nations and to integrating scientifically their institutions into a universal pattern of civilised government.' Nobody can be expected to deny the strength of considerations such as these.

But there are other reasons concerned with the development of political science itself. If we regard our field of study as mainly descriptive, comparisons are required to help us refine our tools of description. If we have hopes of establishing a general theory on an inductive basis, we can do so only through comparison. If we attempt to test specific hypotheses, this is possible only if we bring in a sufficient number of examples, to be investigated by the comparative method.

So much for the reasons in favour of comparative studies. The question of whether or not we should devote ourselves to discussing the *methodology* is a different one. It might be argued—and it sometimes is argued—that there is no point in discussing method. We should simply go ahead and work, and suitable methods will develop without any special effort on our part.

This 'direct' approach is attractive, and we all frequently feel inclined towards it. But further consideration makes it clear that it is not to be taken literally. There are obvious advantages in taking stock, critically, of methods used so far in order to see how they can be improved. In our case this is particularly important since political science and comparative government are not uniformly developed all over the world. In many countries a legalistic or deductive approach still dominates teaching and research, and political science is just coming in. Scholars working there, and coming to their work with an exclusively legal or philosophical training, are eager to make use of the experience of countries where political studies have had a longer tradition, and especially to obviate the necessity of repeating mistakes formerly committed there.

Another consideration should be added. The 'work' achieved is not uniform in value. There must be some standards by which we can judge a piece of research and see whether or not it is worthy of our interest. Both for evaluation and for improvement methodological discussions and studies are useful, not to say indispensable.

On the other hand, it is equally dangerous to misunderstand the character of methodology. There is no *a priori* deductive theory to be developed without regard to the exigencies of actual research and teaching. What we attempt is rather a statement of procedure based on critical observation of work performed so far. While a number of knotty theoretical problems have to be dealt with at various stages, methodology is on the whole intensely practical and not a science in itself.

GENERAL
METHODOLOGICAL PROBLEMS

———

A NUMBER of the problems discussed, both at the Florence meeting and otherwise, are only superficially—if at all—specific to the study of comparative government. Questions concerning the validity of results, the needs of hypothesising, the establishment of a general theory, etc., obviously relate no more to comparative government than to other aspects of political science. In most cases they are common to all social sciences or even to the whole field of humanistic study. Even when we discuss the applicability, e.g., of Mill's method of differences, this is only superficially a specific problem. Whether or not this method is applicable in the field of comparative government depends almost entirely on the general character of results attained in political science.

It would be tempting simply to leave all these questions aside. They seem to be outside the scope of our subject, and in any case we can hardly expect to solve them at this stage. Unfortunately, such a procedure is impossible in view of the present state of discussion. There is no consensus on these points, but rather general disagreement or even confusion. On the other hand, whatever we try to establish with regard to comparative government has to be based on assumptions of a fairly general character. The methodology of comparison is not a self-contained separate subject, but part of the general method of political science. The fundamental assumptions, therefore, have to be discussed even if the results of the discussions are inconclusive and some of the arguments no more than commonplaces.

For political science as well as for other fields of scholarship and scientific study, the fundamental questions are those concerned with truth and validity. Certain aspects can be disposed of rather quickly. It is against the assumptions of Western civilisation to assert that any science can ever be permitted to deviate for any reason from the quest for truth. This should be self-evident and on the whole is so regarded, but we sometimes forget the implications. I quote a paper by Professor Beer of Harvard University: 'In the United States, for instance, it is not uncommon to speak of the teaching of political science as "education for citizenship." Whether one objects to this or not depends on what it means. But on the face of it, the notion seems to me an abomination. I should prefer the premise—vague as it is—that our task is to try to teach the truth—and that means regardless of its possible consequences on society or the state. Conceivably this premise may conflict with the notion that we are "educating for citizenship." In the bad state, the wise man may be the bad citizen. Or indeed, even in a good state, a wise man may choose not to be, in any real sense, a citizen at all.' As a matter of fact, the talk about 'education for citizenship' is probably not as bad as it seems. Those who use it frequently accept the slightly naïve assumption of liberalism that truth will always be triumphant and that the best citizen is he who has acquired the greatest respect for it. But an unsophisticated person may sometimes forget this basic consideration, and where this happens, scientific truth is in danger and scholars may be subjected to witch-hunts.

Another point is concerned less with outside influence than with the psychology of scientists themselves. We all hold a great number of theories and assumptions, on which we base our reasoning. These basic assumptions may or may not be generally accepted. In many cases they are *implicit*, although never expressly stated. It is highly desirable that they should be brought to the surface and made *explicit* to the greatest possible extent, since our reasoning may be unintelligible where this is not the case. On the other hand, we are not always conscious of our own assumptions. Particularly where they seem to us (but not necessarily to others) to be self-evident, they may not at all appear on the surface. This is always a danger, but it is particularly dangerous where we move in an international setting or else under circumstances where it can be suspected that basic differences exist among writers on the same or similar subjects. Consequently, a special effort is required to make implicit assumptions and theories explicit if we are to avoid serious misunderstandings and complications.

This brings us to a more fundamental question, that of *criteria of relevance*. It is sometimes argued that our functions are 'merely descriptive' and that this should relieve us of a number of considerations which might otherwise be necessary. It is submitted that this is an altogether unrealistic assumption. Photographical description is beyond the realm of possibility, if indeed desirable. It is completely impossible to 'merely describe' in the sense of giving 'all the facts': facts and data always have to be selected. Consequently, there has to be a basis of selection. What we mean when we say 'all the facts' is all the *relevant* facts; it remains to set a standard by which we can decide which facts are relevant or not.

This observation has led some scholars to the conclusion that the selection of data has to be based on a previously established general theory. Undoubtedly, this approach is far from impossible in itself. Provided there is a general theory, and provided it is universally accepted or at least universally regarded as of fundamental interest, it can be used as a criterion of relevance. Some of the theories in the physical sciences, such as the theory of relativity, appear to have been successfully used for such purposes.

We may for the moment leave aside the question whether the circumstances of social sciences in general and of comparative government in particular are such as to warrant the employment of this method even under the most favourable conditions. At any rate, it would be a fatal mistake to regard it as the only possible approach. It is equally reasonable and much more simple to regard the question of relevance in the light of particular problems. These problems may be as limited as we like, and it follows that the standard of relevance need not be absolute. Certain data may be irrelevant in connection with one problem but highly important in the light of another. Let us assume that we are collecting data on the activity of cabinet ministers. If our problem is that of the inner mechanism of a cabinet certain facts are important; if we are concerned with parliamentary leadership we concentrate on others. Certain data may be relevant to both problems, particularly since the two are closely connected; but in a majority of cases our choice of data depends on which of the two problems we are concerned with. And for a third problem the social and educational background of ministers, their moral standards, etc., may be of fundamental importance—which leads us to select a third set of data.

The problem of *validity* is of a more basic and fundamental character. In approaching it social scientists in general and political scientists in particular seem to suffer from a hypnotic preoccupation with the exact natural sciences. Physics, mathematics, chemistry, mechanics, are regarded as preeminently scientific and all other scholars are developing an inferiority complex. Consequently, they yearn for measurable quantities, absolute conclusions on causality, etc.

This seems to be particularly true of those who do not have even a superficial acquaintance with natural science. Closer observation should be encouraging. In the first place natural science is not a monolithic block, and all natural sciences are not equally exact. The standards of biology are indeed very far from those of pure mathematics and mechanics. Secondly, largely as a result of recent development, physics and chemistry also deal to a considerable extent with non-measurable quantities and with approximations. The whole field of nuclear physics is a case in point. And finally, the social sciences are not alone suffering from these limitations. We have to accept the fact that all cultural sciences, including history, law, etc., are rather different from the exact natural sciences in this respect. Some fields, such as the very fashionable one of psychology, offer even less hope of exactitude than do the older humanistic sciences.

Consequently, we have to accept the fact that the social sciences are not 'scientific' in exactly the same way and to the same extent as, let us say, physics. In political science, as well as in other cultural sciences, 'scientificness' is hardly more than an attitude of mind. This, of course, does not dispense us from considering critically the reliability and especially the validity of our results. We may hope that in some very distant future we shall be able to obtain a reliability and a validity comparable to those of the exact natural sciences. But since the sciences of man deal with realities which are more complicated than those of the former, it is improbable that this desirable result will come in sight within the near future.

Two solutions would then seem to be possible. Either we have to exclude all problems where such an attitude is at present unattainable—which in practice would mean that we shall have to stop working—or else we have to be content with results which are only very approximate in character. The first proposal has never been advanced, and consequently we are left with the latter.

Thus, we have to accept our own limitations. By the same token, however, we must see that we are conscious of them. We may possibly observe general tendencies, but we cannot expect to find 'laws of political behaviour.' If we promise to do more than we can, we cease to be scientists, but as long as we make it clear to ourselves and to others that our results are imperfect, we may continue to work with a good conscience and make shift with unsatisfactory measures and classifications, hoping that our tools will ultimately improve.

The need for consciousness of our own limitations can

hardly be overemphasised. We may, for instance, establish 'systems' to illustrate our meaning and to list the components influencing developments (or as many as possible of them). We may hope to prove that these components really are important for the result, but we must not assume that we are able empirically to establish the 'weight' or 'value' of each of them. We have to accept that our science is 'descriptive' instead of regarding this as a term of abuse, while obviously attempting to refine our instruments of description—e.g. by comparative studies. And while our observation will, in a certain sense, always remain superficial, this does not prevent us from attempting as much 'depth' as possible in looking for causes as far as possible even beyond those which are immediately apparent.

The attitude just described has much influence on our approach to such things as *predictions*. In a more general way, it even modifies the use of hypothesising.

It might be said that there are sciences of prediction and sciences of explanation; or rather, since science always seeks explanation, that there are certain fields where attempts at explanation may make it possible to predict, and others where this is not the case. This would seem to apply to any statement about the future. The idea that one should distinguish between predictions and forecasts is unintelligible to the present reporter, since general predictions are always made up of specific forecasts and logically lead to other specific forecasts. Any statement about the future, whether of a more detailed or of a more general character, seems to be subject to the same conditions.

Now, the future can be known to us only in so far as the various components influencing events are known to us, not only in the sense that they have all or nearly all been discovered but also, and more particularly, in the sense that we are able to measure them and thus state their relative influence in terms which must not be altogether haphazard, although a certain amount of approximation is permissible. This is what happens in the exact sciences, where deviation from predicted events indicates the presence of an unknown quantity which very frequently is discovered and measured shortly after the deviation has been observed.

In the cultural sciences, this procedure is at present hardly possible. Even where we can find measurements for some of the factors involved, as for instance in the case of public opinion polls, there are always a number of unmeasured and provisionally unmeasurable quantities of real and practically always equal importance. But worse still: even where we deal with 'measurable' quantities, they each have measures of their own which can no more be combined than we are able to perform the traditional feat of adding apples to pears. Take the case just mentioned, public opinion polls. We find that the members of one party are in favour of an extension of the suffrage to persons between 18 and 21 and opposed to government control of water resources; while the members of another party are in favour of government control of water resources but opposed to the extension of the suffrage. Does this tell us anything with regard to the possibility of making a deal between the parties to extend both the suffrage and control of water resources? Obviously not. Even if we have figures for the proportion of party members wanting one thing and another, we are unable to measure the intensity of one wish as compared to another; nor can we be certain that the figures mean the same thing in both parties. Consequently, even where we are able to establish the existence of 'tendencies' of different types and apparently to find some measure of their strength, we have so far no means of comparing them quantitatively and thus to make sure of what is their strength as components influencing events. Since we invariably deal with conflicting tendencies, this seems to make statements about the future completely unreliable except in the exceedingly rare cases where one tendency is incomparably stronger than the others; and these are precisely the cases where prediction is generally possible to any informed person without the use of scientific methods.

The question of *hypotheses* is an entirely different one. The Evanston report[1] placed great emphasis on hypothesising. It said that comparative government had so far been 'insensitive to hypothesising' and insisted that problems should be 'stated in such a form as to lead immediately to hypotheses.' Undoubtedly, the former may be true to some extent and the latter is not impossible, in so far as the hypotheses refer to and are permitted to remain approximative and related only to tendencies.

Yet even here it is impossible to repress certain doubts. On the one hand, the problem has to be posed before the collection of data begins; on the other hand, hypotheses altogether without basis in facts are apt to be somewhat uninteresting. Consequently, we may pose a problem in the hope that it will lead to fruitful hypotheses, only to find when we have got to the facts that nothing of the sort is practically possible. The problem may be interesting in itself, and it may even be useful to pose it, although at the present stage of knowledge we are not able to make even the most tentative hypotheses with regard to the solution.

Furthermore, on the basis of data collected not only our hypotheses, but even the character of our problem frequently change. There is a continual process of mutual influence between the character of the problem and the collection of the facts. Actually, while a general hypothesis is frequently inherent in the problem, what we can demand is hardly more than that any study of the political process—whether comparative or not—should start from a clearly and explicitly stated problem. One has to agree that this has not always been the case in the past.

So far, we have been dealing more or less with problems common to all cultural sciences. It will be necessary to come

[1] *American Political Review*, Vol. XLVII, No. 3, Sept. 1953.

back somewhat farther on to the problem of relationship between various fields, and the meaning of the *inter-disciplinary* approach can not be discussed here. It should, however, be mentioned that while co-operation is indeed necessary and exchange of experiences highly useful, there are definite methodological differences between the cultural sciences. It was said by one of the participants who attended both the Evanston and the Florence deliberations that we should 'use history, but not as historians do.' This applies to all related sciences, including sociology: we should use their results and study their methods but not necessarily copy their jargon.

The place of political science in *relation to other cultural and especially social sciences* is not altogether easy to determine. The unity of science is becoming increasingly evident, and the delimitations are appearing as somewhat futile. Particularly as our work develops the borderline fields grow increasingly important. This, however, does not mean that it is impossible to describe broadly what political science in practice does mean. Indeed, something of this sort is indispensable if we are to attain a coherent and systematic approach to any problems at all.

In a recent paper, Professor S. E. Finer has attempted a general definition of *what is meant by a political predicament:*

'If I insist on red curtains but my wife insists on green—a political predicament exists. If I demand free trade, and others protection—a political predicament exists. If Russia wants a disarmed Germany and the Western Powers wish to rearm her —again, a political predicament exists. In all cases, what *I* wish to do is such as automatically to bind *him* to do something he does not want to do: and what *he* wants to do is such as automatically to bind *me* to do something *I* do not wish to do. The characteristic features of the predicament are identical: in the first place the policies pursued are such as by their nature to eliminate the alternatives (and thus involve their champions' compliance with the victorious policy); and in the second place, no unanimity exists as to which policy should be pursued.

(a) A political predicament does not arise unless there are two or more actors. Robinson Crusoe was not involved in politics until Man Friday arrived. A neat way, therefore, of solving a political predicament is to make sure it does not exist: i.e. by eliminating everybody else.

(b) Nor does a political predicament arise where the policies in question are compatible: for they can be pursued side by side. An untidy but practical way of solving political predicaments is to modify the original, competing policies until they reach this condition.

(c) Nor, finally, does the political predicament arise unless there are two or more policies; i.e. unless there is a lack of unanimity. No competition in policy, no predicament; no predicament, no activity. There is no problem to solve. Sometimes people become bored with this condition. Then they invent predicaments. Such invented predicaments are games and sports, such as cricket, football, boxing matches. They are analogical to politics (as most of our political philosophers, who are usually cricket-mad, do not hesitate to point out).'

If we accept these definitions it is obvious that we are concerned not only with forms but with realities, and with *specific* realities. This is true whatever is the object of our study. For instance, the party system in France may be the object not only of political but also of historical and sociological studies. The political scientist is interested in finding out what are the power relations between the parties and within the parties, as well as between parties and other organised and unorganised groups. His primary interest is concerned with the situation as it stands today, but in order to understand this he will frequently have to go back and look for the genesis of the present state of affairs. He will also have to seek a background in contemporary and recent circumstances outside the field of power relations. To the sociologist, on the other hand, power relations are only one of the interesting factors, and hardly the most interesting. To him agreement is frequently of greater interest than conflict, and his question will be concerned, for instance, with the role of party organisation in the social life of communities, status attainable through the individual's influence within the party, etc. The historian, finally, is interested in all these things, but to him the recent situation is no more important than the situation 200 or 300 years ago. The important thing is what changes have taken place, and why; whether these changes are mainly related to the political aspects of the party system or to something else.

On the other hand, it is also sometimes argued that 'a political scientist covers the same world in the mind that a statesman covers in action'; this signifies that political science is identical with statecraft. This would seem to be rather ambitious, particularly since in the modern world statecraft is concerned with practically all sides of human life; which political science would fain *not* be.

In attempting to discuss the role of methodology, we may refer to certain general problems mentioned in the introduction. In particular, the problem centres round the general objectives of political science. On the whole, an empirical—or, as it is sometimes called, experimentalist—attitude has found pretty general acceptance. Empiricism, of course, is in itself a methodological principle of the first order, but it is sometimes interpreted so as to dispense with discussion of other methodological problems. Empiricism, then, would be regarded as 'a methodology to end all methodologies.' But this interpretation is neither necessary nor entirely reasonable. There is also, on the other hand, a very definite hunger for discussion of methodological principles, and notably so in the United States.

Probably because of the over-emphasis on pragmatism formerly usual on the Western side of the Atlantic, there is in American political science today a great anxiety to get down to fundamentals—just as the formerly more speculative Europeans are anxious to deal with nothing but solid facts.

While the empirical attitude by no means precludes further study of methods, it is obviously true that methods can be developed and tested only by successful research investigations. But which are the criteria of success? It seems that the results should in the first place be coherent and thus reasonably immune to immanent criticism. Secondly, a successful investigation is one where the results are corrected and developed by further study, but not entirely discarded. Finally, it is sometimes held that the success of the investigation is proved by the fact that predictions contained in it prove to be true. This may be open to some doubt: the results may be purely coincidental, while on the other hand an investigation may be highly useful although a minor flaw prevents it from forming the basis of correct prediction. In any case there is undoubtedly a strong correlation between the empirical approach and the establishment of fruitful hypotheses. In the words of S. V. Kogekar: 'An empirical approach to the problems of political science which centre, broadly speaking, round the organisation and control of human relations in society, assumes great importance in this task of hypothesising. Not that hypotheses are always and necessarily the product of empirical studies. But such studies may both stimulate our minds in the task of hypothesising and provide a testing ground for the hypotheses arrived at by whatever process.'

In any case it would obviously be nonsense to say that no methodology is required, while at the same time maintaining that the correct method is proven by the successful result of investigation where it has been applied. The moment we start to speak of *successful* investigation, we are in need of criteria for success. These criteria can be developed only through

methodological discussion, and thus even the extreme empiri-
cist can never avoid consideration of principles in this respect;
he can only lose in clarity by making them implicit and not
explicit.

What 'methodology' is can thus be stated rather simply: to
take stock of methods used so far, criticise them on the basis of
the results attained in employing them and trying to perfect
them further with a view to the future. This is something which
we are all doing, consciously or unconsciously. But it is
particularly for countries where the study of political science
is just beginning that we need to present explicitly our
experiences.

On the other hand, we must remain conscious of the limitations of methodological study. Is it supposed to involve a
theory or a procedure? Both are probably included, but the
inductive approach makes it necessary for us to take special
interest in the procedural side. Furthermore, very few methodological rules are universally applicable. On the whole,
methodology is usually related to a problem or a group of
problems and should be discussed in this context. Methodology
in the abstract is hardly very useful, except with regard to a few
almost self-evident basic principles; but a study of the methods
impressed in a particular investigation or type of investigation
can be exceedingly interesting.

As to the basic 'universal' principles, it is sometimes maintained that nothing has been done so far. This seems highly
surprising. It may be that nothing or almost nothing has been
done by political scientists, but in this discipline, as in so many
others, it is necessary to draw on the philosophers, who have
been anything but unconscious of methodological problems
involved in a study of society. We may go back to the 'common-
sense' philosophers in England in the eighteenth and nineteenth
centuries; to a German philosopher like Windelband or a
Swede like Hägerström; or we may refer to an economist and
sociologist like Max Weber. All these authors will have some-

thing of importance to teach us. This does not imply that the last word has been said, and in particular we are in great need of participation by scientists actively engaged in *using* the methods (such as, incidentally, Max Weber). Still there is much to draw on and it would be a serious mistake to assume that we should start from scratch. In fact, more can probably be gained by testing theories already outlined on the basis of results achieved in practical research than by new attempts to develop theories of method *a priori*. The history of social science methodology is a long and interesting one, providing a fertile ground for the growth of new methodological refinements. The problem is not one of inventing ideas but to find out which ideas can be used in practice.

There is undoubtedly in many fields—again particularly in the United States—a desire for the development of a *general theory in political science*. It is hoped by many scholars, as well as probably by laymen, that political science will develop something of direct use for the solution of the problems of our time. To quote Benjamin E. Lippincott in the UNESCO volume on *Contemporary Political Science*: 'We have had two world wars and a great depression, yet no political theory has been written by political scientists, indicating, on the evidence of the past, that all these things are possible, indeed were very likely. No political theorist saw, before it was clear to all who had eyes to see, the deadly challenge made by Nazism, and then by Communism, on a global scale; none saw the "cold war," nor Communist aggression by satellite powers. No book in theory has been written in America, the home of modern democracy, to make an advance on John Stuart Mill, whose writings are still classic ones on the subject; in fact, no one in England or America has produced since his time an analysis of the principles of democratic government equal to his. . . . We may say, in conclusion, that political theory in America will come into its own when political theorists give up their emphasis on the history of political ideas, and on the descriptive approach to political science. It will come into its own when it reaches beyond empiricism, and employs scientific method after the manner of the great physicists. It will begin to perform the task of which it is capable when political theorists take stock of their field, and determine its chief problems. Political theory will become fruitful when its practitioners consult other branches of learning, as well as other fields of political science, for the purpose of testing the operation of its principles.'[1]

Political science is also sometimes said to 'suffer from indigestion of facts.' Karl Loewenstein wants us to continue in the direction of developing what used to be called in Germany *Allgemeine Staatslehre*. The Evanston seminar was apt to regard the development of a general theory alternatively as the main purpose of comparison or even as a necessary basis for establishment of criteria of relevance. And some scholars hope that political science as well as mechanical science is approaching the stage where it can begin to formulate general 'laws.'

Now, the idea of a 'general theory' is by no means unambiguous. It is sometimes understood to mean a theory of 'the best system of government.' This would imply agreement as to values, since otherwise it is impossible to know what is 'best.' It would also require a development of political science up to the point where one can make almost infallible predictions as to how given institutions will work in a given environment. Such a development, however, is certainly not yet even in sight. Finally, under the existing circumstances, attempts to create a general theory of this type would lead us almost directly back to the speculative political theory of Rousseau, Montesquieu and Locke and obliterate practically every distinction between political science and politics. It is a very natural desire to find a theory which is able to answer these questions; but we should be very unwise were we to give out any hope of fulfilling such desires.

[1] *Contemporary Political Science*, pp. 220 *seq.*, 223.

On the other hand, a general theory is sometimes understood as political philosophy pure and simple. There seem to be certain difficulties in accepting this idea also. At least in so far as comparative government is concerned what we can hope to attain is chiefly what has been called a conceptual framework, giving us the definitions and clarifying the problems with the help of which we should analyse existing political institutions and forces. This is both more and less than a political philosophy. It is less in that it does not attempt an explanation of the real nature of the state or the origins of political relationships; but it is more in that it relates directly to empirical facts and not only to speculation.

A definition given by one of the members of the seminar with regard to a general theory of one particular problem should help to clarify matters. Professor Macpherson, in his paper on political parties, started out as follows: 'By general theory of the party system I mean a statement of the relations, necessary or contingent, between the party system and the purposes of democratic government, and, ultimately, of democratic society. A general theory should be built inductively, but the aim (though not completely attainable) should be to state it deductively, i.e. in principles from which the limits and possibilities of party systems in particular circumstances could be deduced. Are party systems necessary to the purposes of democracy? In what ways are they necessary? What characteristics of form and substance are required in party systems if they are to fulfil those purposes? These are some of the questions that should continually be asked. They have not been asked sufficiently often, or not with sufficient care.'

It should be noted that the emphasis here is on deduction, not on induction. In the words of another participant in the seminar, Professor S. E. Finer, we are making an attempt at 'describing the political possibilities.' Considerable emphasis should be put on the word *describing*: we remain in the humble sphere of description and do not attempt to rise to the more lofty one of speculation. With this limitation, the general theory, and perhaps in particular its component parts, should be highly useful, especially in order to make explicit assumptions or theories which we are always implicitly using.

But it is perhaps important to make one further qualification. Even in the physical sciences the general theory is built up of innumerable problem solutions. It is continually developing, and parts of it are no more than sketchy hypotheses or even question-marks. This seems to be even more true of political science. Unless we know *all* states and *everything* about them, no complete theory will ever be possible. Our general theory will resemble a map where large parts, perhaps the largest, are in white, indicating undiscovered lands and attracting further study. And these further studies will necessitate corrections on the map even of what we regard as comparatively well-known territories, since the borders are long and complicated.

By contrast to those hoping for a complete and infallible theory of politics as an immediate result of our study in comparative government, there are also those who indicate that no general theory should be attempted, let alone permitted to influence our studies. We should not attempt to go by the map, but simply march courageously and practically ahead, noting what we see by the roadside and drawing our own conclusions. But just as the man who starts on a walk without bothering to take a map generally has some sort of an idea in his head as to the character of the territory into which he is going, the political scientist who brags about his lack of interest in general theory frequently has a rather complete theory of his own, although he does not bother to make it explicit. Actually, there a number of theories of which we are all conscious and which are continually influencing our thought. It should be sufficient to mention three of the most important ones.

The classical, much maligned institutional approach is definitely a theory; and it has been developed in this manner and with a number of variations by authors such as Jellinek, Kelsen and Esmein. Its basic assumptions are that institutions have a (legal) life and importance of their own; that human beings are on the whole alike and will react similarly to the same institutions; but that the number of possible combinations of institutional arrangements is unlimited, thus leading to the great differences between countries and peoples. A variation of this idea is that of an 'institutional equilibrium,' comparable to the price theory of classical economics and brought forward for the Florence discussions by Professor S. E. Finer.

The pluralistic approach, with the young Harold Laski as its most well-known proponent, is of course even more definitely a general theory. It was formerly regarded as a mere curiosity, but it is becoming more and more widely accepted by political scientists all over the world. This is an important change in the basic assumptions of political science and in particular of comparative government, and it is largely because of this change that some of the earlier characteristics of political science are being criticised today. For pluralism leads us to recognise the fact that what we have to study is not government alone but politics, including a great number of factors formally disregarded. Among those factors are not only the political parties but also more or less organised groups of a seemingly non-political or at least predominantly non-political type— practically on the whole everything which tends to influence public opinion. Quite clearly, the pluralist has to draw much more on economics and sociology than the institutionalist.

Thirdly, there is the power approach: the study of politics as the study of the nature and phenomena of power. This can be combined with either institutionalist or pluralist assumptions. It has so far been important particularly in the United States, but it is spreading all over the world. It deals with all sorts of political situations, including those arising in institutions other than those which we are apt to call political institutions. On the other hand, it has the advantage of providing us with a point of view which is different from those of other social sciences, with the possible exception of political history.

Occasionally, it is argued that the quest for a general theory is opposed to the 'problem' approach. On consideration, however, it must be obvious that there is no real conflict between the two, in so far as a theory must always be built up of problem solutions and at the same time points to new problems which have to be solved. Only if a general theory is interpreted so as to mean unfounded statements about generalities does it seem to be opposed to the careful and detailed study of separate problems. On the other hand, of course, problem studies are also possible without reference to a general theory of politics as a whole. It is clearly quite reasonable to attempt an investigation of a practical problem in itself, leaving open its relationships to other questions.

In choosing problems for study, we can never avoid the question of criteria of relevance. Even within the framework of a general theory this may be quite a difficult one, since not everything related to the theory is of the same importance. And without a general theory providing the framework of reference, opinions may vary even more as to what is relevant and what is not. There is no difficulty in finding examples of this, and in fact some of the most acrimonious discussions between political scientists have been related exactly to the question of whether certain problems should be regarded as relevant or not. The Evanston report dealt with what it called 'narrow-range' and 'middle-range' problems: an analysis of the relations between the power of dissolution and ministerial stability in parliamentary systems forming an example of a 'narrow-range' problem, whereas the political consequences of rapid industrialisation in underdeveloped areas was cited as an example of 'middle-range' problems. 'Wide-range' problems, presumably, would be those related to the fundamentals of a general theory of politics. Obviously the choice of problems in all the three ranges is almost unlimited, even with a view to comparative government. Already ten years before the Evanston report Karl Loewenstein presented examples of equal interest: 'A genuinely comparative approach should operate freely along trans-national lines. Such problems as political power, leadership (in particular, executive leadership), federalism, civil liberties—whether they have a core of sacrosanctity or are subject to sublimation—are common to every state. Solutions arrived at in one national environment cannot fail to have a bearing on similar situations in one or several other states.' But what should govern our choice of problem?

A specific, 'pragmatic' solution is found in what has been called policy-orientation. The problems chosen by political scientists should primarily be the problems confronting statesmen in actual political life. Thus, political science would, so to speak, work to order and present solutions which could be immediately useful to the development of the respective countries and to mankind as a whole.

There are obvious difficulties to this approach. The most obvious one is that those who formulate policies and thus state 'policy oriented' problems are unconscious of a great many aspects of political life which tomorrow may prove more important than what politicians are considering today and which require much more prolonged study than time will allow if we are working merely to order. There is at least a chance that some of the problems of tomorrow will be brought up for discussion in time, if political scientists are not too much concerned with the immediate problems of today. On the other hand, a fairly close relation to political life itself has its uses. We should compare ourselves to the economists, who in the recent past have been far more closely involved than political scientists in actual political considerations. The need for immediate 'solutions' has sometimes stimulated their work, sometimes proved a hindrance to fundamental research, but more seriously it has sometimes also tempted economists to give some sort of scientific authority to the solutions desired by the holders of political power or, alternatively, by those striving to attain it. Political science would do well to attempt to profit by these experiences in avoiding at least some of the major pitfalls into which economists have been dropping.

One might also consider what could be called 'teaching-oriented' problems. The close relationship between teaching and research means not only that teaching has to build on the results provided by research, but also that teaching very frequently puts the spotlight on fundamental problems or on problems not yet sufficiently elucidated by research. This is particularly true in the field of comparative government. Practically no teaching of political science is possible without continual comparison, and thus the teacher is figuratively speaking always working in front of the map. Unknown areas, whether in the literal sense of the word or in the form of problems left aside by the relevant authors, very quickly become apparent in teaching. In fact, it might be argued that teaching provides a better guide than policy orientation for the discovery of problems to be investigated in the field of comparative government. Yet this is certainly not the answer to our question. Teaching may help us to discover the relevant problems, but it does not provide the criteria of relevance. And we are thus left with the highly unsatisfactory conclusion that these criteria are as yet very arbitrary. Perhaps this is what is meant by those who maintain that the study of politics is 'an art, not a science.'

A final observation might be permitted. It deals with the terms in which we are expressing ourselves. On the whole, political science and politics have the same terminology. There are drawbacks in this apparent simplicity, since the terms of political science frequently suffer from being used as weapons in political discussions. It is tempting to try to develop a separate terminology, sufficiently complicated to deter politicians from using it. This would also demonstrate how 'scientific' we are. In the end, it might be developed so as to lead to great precision by avoiding the vagueness of words in common political usage. On the other hand, attempts made so far have frequently proved more ridiculous than precise. And in any case such terminology can be useful only if it is very carefully standardised and maintained over a really long period of time. A varying and changing terminology is more dangerous the more precise it sets out to be.

CLASSIFICATION, TYPOLOGY, TERMINOLOGY

THE questions just discussed are of general importance to political science. Many of them are not at all specific to comparative government although as important there as in any other field of political study. We pass to another type of question, which in a sense is also of general rather than specific interest, but which requires particular attention here: the problem of classification.

Classification is a necessary condition of comparison. In order to be relevant, comparison must be related to a particular problem, which in this field can hardly be stated except in terms of typology. We have to be certain what we are comparing.

Typology, whether for societies, for states or for institutions, generally appears as a result of extensive comparison. On the other hand, already at an early stage it is implicitly or explicitly present at least in a provisional sense in so far as we are assuming certain types between and within which we are making our comparisons. The problems and hypotheses we are employing are almost invariably related precisely to the question whether or not a society, a state or an institution is 'true to type.' Obviously, we can discover a lot of influence from the ideas of Plato at this point; but even the philosophical materialist rarely remains free from such influences.

How far is classification possible? It is sometimes said, as has just been mentioned, that the study of politics is not a science but an art. This, however, in no way dispenses with classification, nor does it make classification unreasonable. In the study of painting, music or literature, classification also remains indispensable; and it should be noted that this is true not only of the critics but also of the artists themselves. It is impossible to find any artist—painter, musician or author—in modern times who has not gone rather deeply into classifying the various aspects of his art, as shown particularly in the work of his predecessors. The emergence of 'schools' in art as well as in science is sufficient proof of this.

Classification, of course, means much more than the establishment of a terminology. It deals with the actual contents covered by the terms, yet there is always the danger that classification may become dogmatic. It is true that while rough and inaccurate classification may remain useful, further refinements are desirable. It is true that up to a point such refinements are precisely the type of results we hope to gain from our study. But it is extremely dangerous to give to types, classifications and terms a separate existence apart from their contents. This was precisely what was happening in German social science before 1914; and the reaction against authors of this type was, in fact, an unavoidable consequence of the development of inductive methods and empiricism.

Classification, therefore, is only ancillary to our study and creates no realities. The borderline cases are frequently more numerous than the 'typical' ones, and it is both meaningless and ridiculous to speak of one classification as 'correct' and another as 'wrong.' At most, one classification may be more convenient or from a given standpoint more useful than another.

Moreover, while typological refinements are in themselves useful and desirable, this is true chiefly in so far as they mean a development of accepted systems of classification. It does happen in social science, as well as in natural science, that a situation occurs in which existing systems of classification are useless and a completely new typology has to be developed. But this is a comparatively rare occurrence, and on the whole fundamental changes in typological and terminological systems are apt to create confusion instead of avoiding it. This becomes clear as soon as we realise that a typology is neither right nor wrong in itself, but only a tool for clarifying ideas to ourselves and others.

For the reason just mentioned, the question has been raised whether a complete standardisation of typology and terminology would not be desirable, and whether this would not be a fit and proper undertaking for international organisations such as UNESCO. On the other hand, it is argued that this is impossible at least in the present state of development and that attempts in this direction could be successful only were one to standardise not only terminologies and systems of classification, but thought itself—which, of course, social scientists should be the first to resist. A 'newspeak' of social science would probably, it is said, have the same effect as newspeak in Orwell's *1984*. On the other hand, the great number of existing systems and the tendency of ambitious scholars to attempt fame by creating new ones leads to other almost equally serious consequences: confusion in which people are continually discussing without understanding what the other fellow is talking about, and concentration on the differences of formal expression rather than on the contents. For purposes of comparison, where it is almost invariably necessary to draw on studies by different scholars, this problem becomes very vexing indeed, and it certainly does not simplify the introduction of political science into areas where the study has no tradition behind it.

Some principles of classification are of fundamental importance already for the delimitation of the field of study of comparative government in general. It is necessary here to refer back to some points already indicated. What is a political body or situation? Until we have defined that we lack the elementary basis of comparison. Should problems be studied from the point of view of power, with regard to the means used for making decisions and to assure obedience to decisions made? Further, should the point of reference be, specifically, concentration versus dispersion of power? In so far as democracy is at the centre of our investigation, this seems to be unavoidable. But we still have to decide whether we can make use of one of the classical triads, e.g. that of Aristotle or that of Montesquieu, or whether something else is required under the circumstances of modern politics. All attempts at large-scale comparison are based on some general assumption of this type; and those assumptions must be made explicit in the form of definite terms of reference.

When going into more specific problems, we find that the terms of reference for classification depend largely on our choice of problem. The Evanston seminar gave some examples of wide problems, and a study of their list clearly indicates the differences in basic terms of reference which will appear in the several cases:

(1) The setting of politics (an enumeration of the most significant contextual factors of all political systems, i.e. geographical pattern, economic structure, transportation and communication patterns, sociological structure and minorities, cultural patterns, values and value systems, and the record of social change).

(2) The sphere of politics: the actual and potential sphere of political decisions (conditions determining the sphere of decision-making; limits on political decision; major types of decision-making; and potential changes in the sphere of decision-making).

(3) Who makes decisions—the *élite*. (Who are they supposed to be? To whom does the community impute prestige and what are the prevalent prestige images and symbols? Forms of selection of political *élites*—ascription, achievement. Who actually make the effective political decisions if they differ from those who are supposed to make them? By what means? The breakdown of *élites*: regional, etc. Stability of the *élite*. Types

of personal participation in the decision-making process.)

(4) How decisions are made (formulation of problems; agencies and channels of decision-making; decision-making procedure; some major characteristics of decision-making procedure).

(5) Why are decisions obeyed? (The enforcement of decisions; compliance; consent; types of consent; the sociology of compliance; some check-points for the measurement of compliance.)

(6) Practical politics; policy aspiration groups and power aspiration groups. (Policy aspiration groups: types, purpose, organisation, techniques. Power aspiration groups: types, goals, organisation, techniques, influence and effectiveness.)

(7) The performance of the system: stability, adjustment, and change.

(a) Conditions of stability and change (legitimacy myth, relationship between formal and informal processes). Manifestations of instability and stability (legitimacy myth, formal and informal processes). Allocation of decision-making power (leadership); some check-points for stability and instability.

(b) Change (conditions of; manifestation; types; check-points for assessing conditions for potential change.)

In the case of some of the conventional problems of political science this is even more obvious. Take electoral systems. During the Florence discussion Professor Pollock used the following classification:

(1) Single-member district systems—be they either majority or plurality, with a single ballot or a second ballot.

(2) Proportional representation systems—single transferable vote, or list systems.

(3) Other systems—whether based on preferential voting or functional representation or on possible combinations of (1) and (2).

Or take political parties: how far back in history can we talk of parties? What about the groups in the Athenian assembly; the contending factions in Italian cities at the time of Macchiavelli; the connections in England during the eighteenth century? What is a 'two-party system'? Was there such a system in England in the nineteenth and earlier twentieth century or not? Is there a two-party system in the United States today? The answer to all these questions depends on the classifications we use and the definitions which are employed to implement them.

During the Florence discussions considerable disagreement appeared as to what should be meant by a revolution. Is any sweeping change revolutionary in character? Is swiftness an essential factor; is the use of violence an important characteristic of revolutionary change? Is a *coup d'état*, transferring power from one small group to another, essentially distinct from a revolution, and if so, where shall we draw the line separating the two? It is obvious that these questions can be answered in many different ways with equal plausibility, but it is also obvious that unlimited confusion may arise if we use different definitions.

The more modern institutional problems are by no means exempt from these difficulties. A good example of this is the term 'pressure groups.' The word originates in the United States where the most exhaustive studies of these groups have taken place. It is there generally assumed that a pressure group is an extra-parliamentary body working through different political parties. Such an assumption, however, is apt to create confusion rather than clarification in regard to Western Europe, where groups are apt to work through parties and even be affiliated to specific party organisations. On the other hand, there *are* in Europe also groups which are working differently.

In all these cases various systems of classification and typologies might be usefully employed. Reasonable doubts can be held about which system is the best one. But in the last resort it is far less important to argue about which is the better typology than to make it clear to everybody *which* typology is being employed and to avoid novelties which will make reference to earlier studies more difficult.

THE CONFIGURATIVE APPROACH

THERE has been much discussion lately as to whether the approach of political science, and particularly of comparative government, should be analytical or configurative. Here again, we are confronted with a problem which is fundamentally general in its character and by no means specific to the study of comparative government or even to political science. The answer to our question depends on our general assumptions with regard to human society and indeed to human nature as a whole.

So far, there seems to be little or no material to support any general theory permitting us to use either the analytical or the configurative approach to the exclusion of the other. Provisionally, therefore, we shall have to work with both, not with one of them. This means, of course, that we have to make our comparison both in the light of special institutional and functional problems and with reference to what has been called national profiles.

We shall later return to the meaning of the analytical approach. For obvious reasons it lends itself much more easily to detailed discussions than the configurative. A few comments on the latter are, however, indispensable at the present stage.

In the first place, a study of national profiles does not necessarily either presuppose or repudiate the idea of a 'national character.' The national profile is a term referring to the over-all characteristics or sum total of characteristics of a given nation at a given time. These characteristics may be the result of ethnical or even biological conditions, which are not subject to change in their basic features; or they may be simply the result of historical, economic or similar circumstances and thus apt to change gradually if not suddenly when these circumstances are altered. It does not seem necessary for us to make our choice between these two alternatives in order to act on configurative lines. Whether our study deals with a specific situation or with historical development we may at least to start with leave the choice open. Indeed our attitude in this respect will probably be determined by our results rather than condition our study.

There is, however, one point which is closely related to the question of national character and which will appear at various stages of our investigation. This is whether there exists what has been called a 'unity of human society,' that is whether society is fundamentally the same everywhere or whether this is not the case. The idea of such a unity, while sometimes propounded, is not generally accepted. At any rate it is not an axiom but rather a fundamental problem to be investigated by all social sciences, including political science. Such an investigation is possible only by comparative study; that is, by trying to find out whether similar circumstances and factors lead to similar results in different environments. It should be noted that the idea of 'backward' regions or nations is based on these assumptions. In speaking in such terms, we consciously or unconsciously assume that all societies are passing through approximately the same 'stages of development.' Some of them have got a little farther, others have a little farther to go, but sooner or later they will all pass through the same or at least similar experiences. Those who made it their programme 'to make the world safe for democracy,' for instance, assumed that democracy in the British, French and American sense of the word was in itself not only a 'higher' stage of development than feudalism or autocracy but also a stage which in the normal run of things should be reached sooner or later by all peoples on earth.

Attitudes of this type are now becoming less and less common. Even with regard to the highly developed areas of the West, it is more and more generally accepted that we have to take into account the 'context'; that is, deal not only with particular institutions, but also with the total character of the society in which the institution is placed, and that the same institution does not necessarily mean the same thing in a different context. This was very clearly set out in a paper contributed by Professor Herman Finer for the Florence meeting:

'How perseveringly it is necessary to relate society and state may be appreciated by a brief reflection on two other problems. Supposing we asked what lessons can be drawn from British experience for the conduct of an "opposition" in the United States Congress. To be more exact, what advice could be given to an American who is in a leading position for nomination as presidential candidate three or four years hence, he not now being in any office? On reflection, he would seriously harm his prospects if he took up the responsibilities of a leader of the opposition in the British parliamentary system. Even acting in the most noble spirit of constructive opposition, he would draw on himself all the ignominy of cavilling and carping from people who want a quiet life, the jealousy of less gifted members of his party in and out of office, and accumulate so much rancour, heaped high by the press, that he would spoil his chances of nomination. Why? Because the parties are flabby and split, his own would not rally round him, and they are so because American society—the environment, the wealth, the regional diversities, and other causes—keep them so. He would be tripped up by rivals in his own camp. The best advice is to keep quiet, let other people commit themselves and get slapped, and emerge only in the fourth year for a drive for the nomination and then another for the Presidency—but never to expose the flank to the charge that one is criticising unconstructively and without responsibility. The public that wants to eat well and chew gum does not like this.

'Let us take another example. It would do France good to have a fixed Executive like the American Presidency. But until some disaster threatens the nation, that will not be instituted. The national experience from ancient times down to 1870 has been for the French nation to receive hurt from the Executive, with a repetition of evil (in the opinion of the majority), between 1940 and 1944, under Marshal Pétain. They would contrive to weaken a fixed Presidency as they have managed to make practically nothing but a figurehead of the President of the Republic and an Aunt Sally of the Cabinet at the mercy of the missiles thrown at it by the National Assembly.

'In all this—and the hypothetical answers are not put forward as true at this stage—one may learn perhaps what is alterable and what is unalterable. Perhaps one may be stimulated to imagine what might be done to modify or compensate for the evils (if they are regarded as such) of what is too rooted and firm to be changed, and the best feasible fulfilment of what is open to reform.'

If this is true with regard to Western countries, which have for a long time been mutually influencing each other, it is even more so with regard to the 'new' or 'underdeveloped' areas which have been subject to cultural exchange with the West only sporadically and chiefly on the surface. There, context means even more. This idea was brought out forcibly in one of the comments on the report of the Evanston seminar (by Ralph Braibanti):

'There is another reason why any study of Asia which ignores the total fabric of society is likely to be unproductive. This is simply the uniqueness of many of the externals of Asian government. The problem does not arise in quite the same way when governments of the West are compared. France has its *Conseil d'État*, it is true, but both England and the United States have highly developed bodies of administrative law even though they lack an independent juridical structure for its administration. Often the distinctions of the West are distinctions of degree rather than kind. But where in the West (aside from the *mir* of Russia, which itself probably has Asiatic antecedents) can we find anything remotely similar to the system of collective neighbourhood responsibility found in the *chia-pao* of China, or the *tonari-gumi* of Japan? There is nothing in our own system to which these institutions can be compared. But careful analysis of the factors giving rise to these institutions may lead to significant hypotheses. Certainly the idea of the Chinese censorate (found in the Chinese constitution and reflected in Japanese government) cannot be productively compared to anything in the West (not withstanding the fact that both Vermont and Pennsylvania had councils of censors for a brief period). Risking facile generalisation, analysis of the culture would probably reveal that censors were necessary because of the broad discretion allowed Chinese and Japanese administrators. This trust of the administrator in turn is probably due to Confucian optimism about the essential goodness of man and the particular virtue of the educated official. This kind of analysis requires intimacy with the writings of Confucius, Lao-Tse, Mencius and others. Thus the spiral spreads to include the ideas held sacred by the people.'

The meaning of this should be abundantly clear. If, for instance, we use a problem such as that of concentration versus dispersion of power as our term of reference, only extensive knowledge of the context, that is of the general social and political configuration, makes it possible for us to see whether the 'same' institution really means the same thing in two societies, or whether such things as universal suffrage, parliamentary responsibility, etc., lead to basically different results.

Using the configurative approach in political science, then, means that we base our comparisons on a study of the political system as a whole, not only of particular institutions. But in fact it takes us much farther. We cannot stop at political institutions only but must make use of an interdisciplinary approach. Economic, social, religious and other cultural factors have to be brought into the picture at once, and psychological attitudes prevailing in different societies are perhaps the basic consideration, leaving open the question whether these attitudes are exclusively created by environments or have other, more fundamental causes. By this means we may possibly in the end reach some understanding of what national 'profiles' or national 'character' are, avoiding the superstitions frequently attached to such terms.

ANCILLARY FIELDS OF STUDY

IN the report by Professor Robson[1] on the teaching of political science, one chapter was devoted to the question of what subjects can be most effectively associated with political science for teaching purposes. Undoubtedly, the same problem arises with regard to research. It is a problem of general importance touching on the relationship of 'different sciences,' not only in the social field, but in all fields of knowledge. But it is especially important when we are attempting comparison, not only for the reason already mentioned in connection with the configurative approach, but also because comparison is in itself an interdisciplinary, perhaps rather a non-disciplinary problem. It therefore requires attention at this point.

It is probably more or less generally accepted that there is something which may be called the unity of science. We cannot think of economics, sociology, political science, cultural anthropology, any more than of chemistry, mechanics, biology, etc., as a group of self-contained units, each clearly defined and independent of the others. We must rather think of science as a field of study which for practical purposes we have to divide between us, but which in principle is a whole, not a group of separate parts. Moreover, strict delimitation between the different parts of the field are not only difficult but also futile. There is no point in spending time and effort on deciding whether a given problem belongs to one or another of the sciences: the main thing is to study it and as far as possible to solve it.

In this sense, the interdisciplinary approach is always

[1] *The University Teaching of Political Science* published by UNESCO.

unavoidable. On the other hand, there are undoubtedly certain questions falling traditionally and unquestionably within the focus of interest of a given discipline. For instance, parliamentary government is studied in political science and neither in economics nor in sociology. The price mechanism falls in economics; and studies of how people use their spare time are of interest chiefly to sociologists. But the border-line problems, such as the attitude of electors to pressure groups and parties, the effect of economic crises on social behaviour, and the attitude of families towards the demand for various commodities are coming into the foreground. The more we find it necessary to deal with problems of this type, the more we are forced to make use of the interdisciplinary approach, considering that the past performances of no particular social science equips it to deal by itself with questions of this type.

In comparative government, the interdisciplinary approach is necessary for other reasons also. We find ourselves in close relationship with other social sciences, taking the word in its widest sense. We are all of us making comparisons, and in doing so we have to assimilate not only the experience but also the accumulated knowledge of other sciences, since these may explain a number of the things which are puzzling us.

Consequently, the study of comparative government requires extensive use of 'ancillary sciences.' It should be made clear that these are by no means 'ancillary' in themselves, but only in relation to the particular approach which we are using at the moment. Just as one field of political science may be 'ancillary' to another—constitutional history to comparative government or comparative government to constitutional history—and as comparative government may hope to be of assistance to the development not only of political theory but also of sociological theory, so in this case sociology or economics are drawn to the assistance of the study of comparative government. There is no question of subordination here. It was only in medieval universities that certain fields of study were held to be superior to others.

If we see the question in this light, certain conclusions can be drawn as to how the interdisciplinary approach is to be interpreted. In making use of other sciences than our own we frequently have to apply their *results*. In many cases we are studying one aspect of certain *data* or *problems*, another aspect of which is being studied elsewhere. It is also useful to see what *methods* are being used elsewhere. The latter, however, can be done only if we are conscious of the fact that the 'difference' between various sciences is frequently to be found chiefly on the methodological plane. While we have to study with great interest how others are approaching problems similar to our own, we must not assume that their methods can be uncritically applied to our own field. This was the basis of some of the criticisms levelled during the Florence meeting at the report of the Evanston seminar. It was felt that this report was too much filled up with 'sociological jargon' attempting to bring comparative government within the *categories* of sociology, instead of using whatever sociological knowledge we may have within the categories of political science. In a sense this may be called a superficial criticism just as some of the criticism expressed in the Evanston report was superficial. Yet it is a limitation to the interdisciplinary approach which must not be forgotten.

In mentioning specific examples of sciences 'ancillary' to the study of comparative government it should first of all be emphasized that the field of choice is unlimited. If we are studying the political implications of the use of atomic energy, we must draw on nuclear physics. If we are going into political semantics, we have to draw on philology as well as on individual psychology. And quite obviously these are fields lending themselves to comparative study. Every scholar will have experienced the fact that he is on occasion suddenly compelled to acquire the most esoteric knowledge before he can make any progress at a particular point. But in discussing the general aspect of the interdisciplinary approach as relating to comparative government, it is probably useful to limit ourselves to the fields which are most frequently important. And these are not necessarily the same as those important in other fields of political science. For instance, philosophy is, very frequently, almost incessantly drawn upon by political theory, but only very rarely by comparative government.

Let us begin with *history*. This is traditionally important, although there is at present a tendency, very much lamented by this reporter, to disregard it. Why and how is it important, except in the sense that our data are always historical since they are undergoing rapid change? As we shall see later, one of the difficulties in making comparisons is that we have so many variables but relatively few examples which we are comparing. If we draw on the experiences of different periods, for instance, in the case of parliamentary government on the United Kingdom in the seventeenth, eighteenth and nineteenth centuries as well as in the twentieth, we find ourselves with many more examples without any appreciable increase in the number of variables. Also, we can make use of the tradition of earlier political thought to draw on the experience of states no longer in existence, such as Athens, Rome, the Ottoman Empire, etc. From the point of view of comparative government also, archaeology is no mean part of history.

We must, of course, make certain reservations. Our problems are not always the same as the problems of the historians. Also, for certain purposes history does not provide us with the data which we need. In a paper for the Florence conference Professor Macridis mentioned an example of this: 'Let us take the multi-party system in France. The historian studying French political institutions will describe the origin, development and ideological and institutional factors of the French multi-party system. The student of comparative politics faced with the same problems should ask the following question: What are the conditions for the existence of a multi-party system? Are they institutional? Social? Sectional? Ideological? Once the conditions have been identified, then comparison with other multi-party structures will show the relevance of some but not others, i.e. comparative study may disprove the relationship between certain conditions and multi-partism. We may find, for instance, that analogous sectional conditions in the United States have not produced a multi-party system. Or that a similar electoral system exists in given two-party and multi-party systems.' In this case, the remedy was obvious. But what is to be done about parties during the French revolution, or, worse still, in ancient Athens? We should note, however, that these are practical and not methodological difficulties. It is not correct to say that we should 'use history but not as historians do,' for the historians are in principle interested in *all* aspects of data and developments, including our own, but not excluding a number of others.

The next traditional field to be mentioned is that of *law*. In many countries political science is still regarded as a part of legal studies and comparative government as a part of the study of comparative law, to be pursued by scholars with a legal training. This is a difficulty for political science as a whole, since the aspects and approaches tend to differ, but it is not more important for the study of comparative government than for any other area of political study. For particular purposes such as a study of the role of the judiciary in government, legal knowledge is indispensable. But moreover, the role of the legal system as a whole is a factor of primary importance for the study of political institutions. A comparison between the approaches of law and politics at this point is highly illustrative. To the jurist, constitutional and political practices are of interest in so far as they form part of or at least influence the legal system (and *mores*). To the student of comparative government, on the other hand, the legal system is important in so far as it forms the basis of certain influences on political developments. It is too frequently forgotten that the study of law may explain differences of political structure and development which otherwise may seem extremely puzzling to us. Other important examples of this are found in comparative administration. Such things as the justiciability of civil servants, the legal means of safeguarding citizens' rights, etc., are fundamental to the understanding of how administration works. But in themselves they are almost unintelligible except in the context of the legal system as a whole.

Next, *economics*. The materialistic conception of history can today be said to be in part accepted by all scholars in the Western world but *in toto* by none. No elaborate argument is required at this point. It is sufficient to mention such examples as the occupational pattern, the distribution of wealth, the dynamic or static character of economic life, industrialisation, etc. No student of comparative government would today venture to leave out such points as these in making his comparisons.

On the other hand, there may be some doubts as to how far we should go. It is undoubtedly dangerous to leave out the results of working of the institutions we are studying. At the Florence conference this point was made by Professor Robson with regard to nationalised industries:

'Lastly comes the task of attempting an evaluation of nationalised industry. This is a matter of extreme difficulty for two reasons. One is that the criteria of efficiency of nationalised industry have never been formulated. Whatever they may be, they are certainly complex and difficult to ascertain.

'Without venturing to formulate a definition of efficiency, I would suggest that in attempting to assess the success of a nationalised undertaking we may inquire into (*a*) output, both aggregate and *per capita*, over a series of years; (*b*) the state of labour relations and of morale; (c) the effect of nationalisation on the distribution of wealth; (d) the degree of public accountability of the undertaking; (e) the price and quality of the commodity or service; (f) development policy; (g) financial results; (h) consumer opinions about the undertaking; (i) its effects on the total economy. . . . Wherever possible, information on these matters should be compared with similar data relating to foreign countries, regardless of whether their corresponding industries are under private or public enterprise. Often, of course, conditions vary so much (e.g. coalmining) in different countries that no common measures can be applied, but this is not invariably the case.'

On the other hand, aims such as these can frequently not be attained if we do not pass from the methods of political science into those of economics, since a comparison in terms of evaluation can hardly take place if we do not enter on both economic theory and economic policy.

Lastly, *sociology*. It is necessary to stress the enormously growing importance of sociological study to the study of comparative government, chiefly caused by the fact that sociology is no more speculative but is entering on an intensely inductive study of society. The importance of a number of sociological factors was continually emphasised during the discussions in Florence, and indeed we are being brought back to a study of the fundamental relationship between state and society. Also, the application of pluralist concepts brings the importance of sociology into the foreground. At every point of our comparison we find examples of this. If we study revolutions we have to take into account their social as well as their political causes as appearing in different environments. If we go into analyses of political parties, we are immediately confronted with their relationship to social classes. We attempt to study the basic democratic mechanism, and we meet with difficulties to be solved only by a study of the sociology of the electorate. We try to follow the political reactions of nations to similar situations, and we are confronted with the influence of religion. We are taking an interest in the development of the political process in a partly illiterate people, and we must take into account the social implications of the educational system. There are innumerable other examples, some of which may in fact prove equally or even more important and elucidating. One of the great contributions of modern American political science is, in fact, that it is proving, largely thanks to characteristics of university organisation in the United States, the extent to which co-operation with sociology is possible as well as indispensable to political science in general and especially to comparative studies.

The four main fields mentioned here are obviously not the only ones. Let us mention in passing a number of disciplines adjoining sociology, such as social psychology, social anthropology and comparative religion. The latter is not the least important, especially when we are approaching new 'areas' where the role of Islam, of Buddhism, of Shintoism, etc., is even more fundamental to politics than that of Christianity in Western Europe of today. Let us also not forget individual psychology, although the data which can be submitted to analysis by the psychologists are insufficient, so that we may be led to unwarranted and unscientific generalisations. In each case it is only one thing we can do, and that is simply to try to find out where we can get assistance in dealing with a particular problem of political comparison.

There is one final remark to be made. It is probably not sufficient for us just to sit down and expect the representatives of 'ancillary' sciences to provide us with the 'results' we need. We must also be prepared to ask questions of our colleagues in other disciplines. This is of mutual interest. The answers may be useful to us, and the questions may be useful to them. Similarly, we may hope that they will have equally useful questions to ask of us. Comparative studies lend themselves most particularly to interdisciplinary teamwork. Comparisons across not only national and cultural but also disciplinary lines will help all sides in posing new questions and finding new answers.

THE TEACHING OF
COMPARATIVE GOVERNMENT

―――――

WE have referred already in the introduction to the study on
the teaching of political science prepared by Professor Robson
and published by UNESCO. Here, of course, a number of
problems applying to comparative government as well as to
other fields of political science are discussed. All the same it
seems necessary to correlate in the present report, also, problems
of teaching to problems of research with special reference to
comparative studies.

This is particularly true because in practice comparison is
more indispensable in teaching than at any other point. Even
if we should dispense completely with all conscious comparison in our research, we could never dispense with it in
teaching. At practically every point, the instructor in government and politics, even at or below the initial level of academic
studies, has to make use of a comparative technique. In dealing
with the institutions and phenomena of other countries, he
has to compare them with those of the students' own country.
And even when dealing exclusively with the latter he must
bring out the salient points by showing how such and such
an institution or a phenomenon differs from those appearing
elsewhere. The consequence is that the whole of our attitude
to comparative studies has been coloured by the requirements
of teaching. This may or may not be a good thing; but any-
how it is so and we have to take it into account from the outset.

Now it is a trite observation that teaching breeds research,
in the particular field with which we are dealing just now as
well as in any other. Whoever attempts to make comparison
in teaching will feel very acutely the need for research and

studies providing him not only with isolated facts about a number of countries, but also with analyses of their interdependency and of the causes and explanations of apparent similarities and differences. But on the other hand it is equally self-evident that comparison in research calls for more 'depth' than comparison in teaching. Both the teacher and the researcher have to leave a number of questions unanswered, but while the former has every right and reason to pass lightly over a number of things as yet unknown, it is the business of research above all to extend the limits of our knowledge and point out the fields which are as yet unexplored.

At the same time, we may usefully stop to consider why comparison is particularly necessary in the teaching of political science, while apparently far less important even in other social sciences. Some of the explanation is given to us if we refer back to what was said at the outset about the study of politics being a quest for truth while being continually exposed to demands to provide 'preparation for citizenship' in a given state or society. This makes it particularly necessary permanently and continually to go on asking questions. Without comparison, we are apt to take things for granted which we find in our own country. To choose some comparatively innocuous examples: the American accepts the federal system, the Frenchman the centralised system of administration and the Englishman the majority system of election as perfectly natural and unavoidable—until the American is brought into contact with large unitary states, the Frenchman with federalism and the Englishman with proportional representation. Then, and only then, can they begin to consider the specific implication of characteristics such as the ones just mentioned.

But even when brought into contact with the phenomena of other states and societies, we are apt to react in an oversimplified manner. Our immediate question is whether what we find elsewhere is 'good' or 'bad.' Students no less than the man in the street are apt not only to put questions in this very simple manner but also to take it for granted that what is similar to their own institutions is 'good' and what is different is 'bad.' The American feels that monarchy is preposterous: surely all civilised people ought to have a republican form of government! To the Englishman proportional representation seems equally unreasonable: has not the parliamentary system worked for more than a century in Britain with a system of majority election, while no country with proportional representation shows a similar record? It is only when we start to make real comparisons that we can begin to understand the relativity of accepted values and standards.

Otherwise expressed: the teaching of comparative government, or perhaps rather the use of comparison in teaching government, enables students to get below the surface and understand the 'realities' of government, thus giving them also a new understanding of the institutions of their own country. It encourages them to see problems rather than be cocksure about solutions. By the same token, it encourages hypothesising on the part of more advanced students. If a general theory is to be presented, illustrations are required if the theory is to be anything but purely abstract dogma. And illustrations can be provided only by the use of a comparative method.

This, however, brings us to the question of *how* comparative government should be taught. There has been some criticism recently of the 'country-by-country approach.' It has been stated that a presentation of several countries, whether in a teaching course or in a textbook, does not constitute comparison, and that therefore much more emphasis should be put on the methodology of comparison itself. There is undoubtedly something in these criticisms. All the same they seem to disregard the fact that any teaching concerned with several governments almost automatically becomes comparative. Where this is not true in the case of the textbook it none the less appears in the teaching course. On the other hand, the comparative approach is often merely implicit and there are good reasons to demand that it be brought to the surface, at least to the extent of constant comparison with the students' own country. For the same reason, studies of the students' own country should take account of the possibilities of comparison. To quote a member of the Florence seminar, Professor Beer: 'The study of the government of one's native country should not be divorced from the study of comparative government, but, on the contrary, ought to be central to it. Perhaps many courses now offered under the heading of Comparative Government in the United States are in fact taught in the light of American experience. I suspect, however, that the separation of "Comparative Government" from "American Government," which appears in most announcements of courses, carries over into the way the courses are taught.'

In fact, while comparison has to be used at every stage there seems to be agreement that basic studies and basic courses have to be organised on country-by-country lines and that it is only at a more advanced level that the comparative method can dominate teaching. For without the basis provided by a knowledge of a number of separate countries, students cannot have the familiarity with various national institutions which alone can enable them to start making comparisons of their own. The data have to be given to them before they start employing the comparative method. This is especially true if we put any value on the configurative aspect of comparison. Students must know sufficiently about the general set-up of different nations and countries before they can begin to understand what specific phenomena mean in a particular environment as compared to another. Also, in making functional comparisons—for instance in the field of parliamentary procedure or electoral method—there will always be a tendency to put an exaggerated emphasis on particular details unless the general position of the institution in question is considered together with its specific characteristics.

The country-by-country approach is therefore a necessary prelude to direct comparison, even if it by no means excludes a gradual introduction of comparative elements into the study of institutions of various countries. At the next stage, area studies are necessary. As has been recently stated,[1] the area concept has frequently been abused in the organisation of university studies. These abuses will be discussed later on; but it cannot be denied that they imply certain difficulties in the use of the concept. All the same, it is useful from a practical point of view, if employed with sufficient caution; and especially so for teaching purposes. Students can hardly be expected to devote time to a study of *all* important countries; they are apt to concentrate on countries within the range of their previous knowledge; and their selection frequently involves the risk that important parts of the world may be left out altogether. Finally, while no two countries are completely alike, and while it is by no means certain that adjoining countries are similar in their institutions, there are undoubtedly certain geographically determined groups where similarity is sufficient to warrant presentation in the form of 'area studies.' In a sense the area approach presents an intermediate stage between the country-by-country approach and attempts at more sweeping comparative studies.

It should be noted that the area study does not necessarily have to be limited to 'new' areas or even to groups of countries very different or distant from that of the students' own country. On the contrary, from the pedagogical point of view there can be good reasons for employing it initially with particular reference to areas which are comparatively well known to the students and perhaps even include their own country. Thus, French or Belgian students may profitably begin with an area study of, let us say, France, Belgium, Holland and Western Germany; Scandinavian students with

---

[1] *American Political Science Review*, Vol. XLVII, No. 2. September 1953, pp. 653 *seq.*

the four Nordic countries; and British students with the senior members of the Commonwealth. In areas of this type comparisons are relatively easy to make, since the similarities greatly outweigh the differences, at least in so far as the general cultural background is concerned.

Finally, at a more advanced stage pure functional comparison can take place. Studies can be made of such things as the organisation and working of the executive branch of government, of parliamentary procedure, of the administrative system, or of the role of political parties in a great number of countries, representing different cultural types. At this stage, also, the interdisciplinary approach has to be introduced, in order to enable students to begin making what may be called vertical comparisons; that is, comparisons concerned with the interdependence of various factors of government. But even at the advanced stage, comparative studies have to be developed gradually, so as to enable students to keep continually in mind the need for a combination of the configurative and the analytical method.

The considerations mentioned in this section are mainly pedagogical and thus concerned chiefly with teaching and not with research. But in so far as teaching is to be considered as the 'mother' of research they should probably have a certain influence on the techniques to be employed in comparative studies for research purposes. The collection of at least a considerable quantity of data concerning different countries and areas is a necessary preliminary not only to conclusions but also to hypothesising. It is true that mere fact-finding without hypotheses is dull and pedestrian. But it is equally true that hypothesising without a factual basis is nothing more than metaphysical speculation. This comes out forcibly when we are confronted with the practical needs of teaching comparative government, but it applies to research as well as to teaching.

THE PRINCIPLES OF COMPARISON

THERE is a common observation which, although trite, is very relevant to the study of comparative government, namely that some of the most outstanding works by political scientists have been prepared by observers writing about a foreign country, although one which they knew comparatively well from practical experience. The classical examples of Bryce, Lowell and de Tocqueville are frequently mentioned, but it is important to remember that they are by no means unique. On the contrary, many similar instances are being produced all the time, and it may be permitted to mention as one of them J. J. Robbins's study of *The Government of Labor Relations in Sweden.*

The obvious reason is that while one may consciously make a study of one's own country entirely without comparisons with others and while studies frequently involve rather little comparison, it is practically impossible to study a foreign country without continually comparing it at least with one's own, but probably also with other countries within one's range of knowledge or experience. Moreover, in studying foreign countries one is apt always to compare them with some sort of an ideal, whether that ideal be the perfect state as envisaged by classical authors or the perfect state which the confident nationalist sees in the institutions of his own country.

If this observation is correct—and it is at least widely accepted—there seems to be good reason to react against the disparaging remarks recently made about the study of foreign government taking the place of the study of comparative government. Not only from the point of view of providing the necessary data, but also with regard to actual, if limited, comparison, the study of foreign governments is of considerable value and interest.

Still, it is necessary to get beyond this limitation. We may refer here to the very apt quotation from Edward Freeman which was brought to mind by one of the participants in the Florence meeting: 'By comparative politics,' he wrote, 'I mean the comparative study of political institutions, of forms of government. And, under the name of Comparative Politics, I wish to point out and bring together many analogies which are to be seen between the political institutions of times and countries most remote from one another. . . . We are concerned with the essential likeness of institutions and we must never allow incidental traits of unlikeness of institutions to keep us from seeing the essential likeness.' Or we may refer to what was said in the report of the 1944 research panel on comparative government when its rapporteur spoke of 'the attempt made really to compare political institutions and functions in the sense that a common denominator for diversified phenomena is found and deviation from the standard pattern is explained.' Comparative government, then, involves *conscious* comparison. To make the objectives and conditions of comparison explicit is one of the main characteristics, and this is a problem in itself even if we leave aside the problem of validity always involved in bringing implicit assumptions and objectives to the surface.

We must therefore focus our attention on the method (or at least the procedure) of comparison. As has been stated already, the country-by-country approach can involve conscious comparison, and not least so in the case of comparison between one's own government and that of other nations. In some respects the difference becomes one of degree rather than of essentials. How many different cases are we attempting to draw into the comparison? Is the comparison focused on one of the cases or does it attempt to treat them all on the same level? The difficulties of comparison are unquestionably greater, the smaller the number of cases studied, since we are dealing with a very great number of variables. The danger of the 'compare-as-you-go' procedure is not only that it is often unconscious, but also that it very generally includes fewer cases than would have been desirable and possible.

For this reason, a minimum requirement for comparison is that it should be based at least on a *conceptual framework,* that is, a number of conscious and consciously interrelated concepts which are applied to the cases brought into comparison.

But it is to be remembered that comparison of this type is not necessarily comparison between different countries or nations. There are also possibilities of comparing different institutions of a similar type within the same country, such as, let us say, political parties, labour unions and co-operatives. Comparison between, for instance, the democratic process used in each of these organisations may in several aspects be just as interesting as comparison between parties, unions and co-operatives separately but in a number of different countries. And it is simplified by the fact that the cultural and social background is on the whole the same, thus relieving us of the necessity of taking some of the most confusing variables into consideration. As a matter of fact, in attempting to develop the methodology of comparative government, studies of this type would probably prove exceedingly useful, if less spectacular than those attempting to cover the surface of the earth in the study of a given institution or group of institutions.

Comparison, of course, always requires *abstraction*. But abstraction needs a firm and definite basis. This basis may be found in policy-oriented terms of reference, in more or less arbitrarily chosen criteria of relevance for the selection of data, or in otherwise determined hypotheses. The 'problem approach' can take many different forms, but it is undoubtedly true that comparison is not sensible unless it is based on a clearly understood problem which is brought up for solution.

The area approach is not an exception to this rule. In studying a given area, one has to pose definite problems just as much as in studying the world as a whole.

On the other hand, one must not require too much refinement in this procedure. At least provisionally, it should be repeated that very rough and unsatisfactory classification may prove useful, and in fact refinement is frequently possible only when the process of comparison is already rather far advanced. This is particularly true in the case of great and sweeping problems, such as that of concentration versus dispersion of power. The more limited the problem is, the more easy does it generally prove to find exact classification and hypotheses at the outset. What is difficult when it comes to the democratic process as a whole is comparatively easy in a study of, let us say, the executive branch of government in cities with over 1,000,000 inhabitants.

Some reflection has recently been given to the possibility of applying to the study of comparative government the principle of the single variable, that is of trying to eliminate from one's material all points of difference with one single exception and to see what is the effect of differences in that particular respect. This is a method which has been successfully applied in the mechanical sciences, but it is submitted that refinements of this type are inconceivable in the study of comparative government. When used in the former, the method is almost invariably based on carefully and severely controlled experiments. But even assuming that some enlightened despot in a completely totalitarian state would permit a group of political scientists to make experiments of this type, it is difficult to say how they could be organised as long as they were dealing not with robots but with human beings, however carefully inoculated and subjugated. We must therefore accept as unavoidable the fact that our comparisons cannot even approach the exactitude of the comparative method as applied in the mechanical sciences.

It has been pointed out that 'two elements are essential to the comparison: (1) a fundamental similarity (technically, an "isomorphism") between the two objects to be compared; and (2) a description of resemblances and differences between the similar elements in the two objects compared. Without the first element, the second is meaningless. There is a famous story about a debate between two eminent comparative anatomists as to the relative size of the spleen in the rabbit and the whale. Their heated conversation was overheard by a classical scholar who turned to them and said: "But Gentlemen! Aristotle says that the whale *has* no spleen." He turned out to be right, and this ended the discussion of the comparative anatomy of spleens.' This argument is completely convincing, if hardly original. But this leaves us with the eternal problem: what is a *relevant* isomorphism; and what is a relevant difference? It is perhaps at this point that we have to be especially careful to state explicitly our assumptions and hypotheses. In fact, one of the fundamental principles of comparison—as opposed to mere description—is that there must be complete clarity as to what particular characteristics are taken into account. On the other hand, we are always confronted with the problem of how to attain sufficient knowledge of data to carry on our comparisons. This is another variation of the aforementioned difficulty that we can produce no general theories unless we know all states; and some political scientists may feel that for this reason it is meaningless to study comparative government at all. Actually, however, it all depends on what results we expect to reach. There is no impossibility at all as long as we are satisfied with inconclusive and temporary results; on the other hand, such results are by no means devoid of interest. Moreover, they gain in validity and therefore also in interest with every increase in the quantity of data forming the materials of comparison—for instance, if we call history to our assistance and compare not only existing institutions but also those of former times.

Some examples were given at the Florence meeting of the *errors* which may at worst appear in the application of the comparative method:

'There is a passage from Bryce[1] which by its naïve self-confidence illustrates this difficulty so well that it must be quoted. He is talking of his *"Method of Enquiry."* And he says:

' "This mode of investigation is known as the Comparative Method. That which entitles it to be called scientific is that it reaches general conclusions by tracing similar causes, eliminating those *disturbing influences which, present in one country and absent in another, make the results in the examined cases different in some points while similar in others.* When by this method of comparison the differences between the working of democratic government in one country and another have been noted, *the local or special conditions, physical or racial or economic, will be examined so as to determine whether it is in them that the source of these differences is to be found. If not in them, then we must turn to the institutions,* and try to discover which of those that exist in popular governments have worked best. . . . When allowance has been made for the different conditions under which each acts, it will be possible to pronounce, upon the balance of consideration, which form offers the best prospect of success. . . ."

'Which, among the multiplex social phenomena of a country wherein it differs from a second country, is Bryce to select as *"the* disturbing influence," which among the multifarious "local or special conditions, physical or racial or economic"? Why does he select some factors and not others? Why has he stressed (say) the religious rather than the economic differences, the geographical rather than the linguistic, and so forth. Bryce must have worked from his own subjective, empirical views of what affected what, and in what degree: but a pre-

[1] *Modern Democracies*, 1921, pp. 20-1.

conceived view of general interrelationships he must have possessed.

'I think this matter can be made still clearer by taking what is perhaps the *locus classicus* of the abuse of the Comparative Method—I mean Lecky's *Democracy and Liberty*.[1] Lecky sets out to prove that the coming of manhood suffrage in Britain by the Reform Act of 1884 must inevitably produce (1) governmental extravagance; (2) corruption; and (3) interference with private property and liberty. His method is to postulate (like Bryce) "similar results...similar causes." The United States are democratic: France is democratic: Britain is (now) democratic —this is the "similar cause." What of the similar results? France is extravagant: Britain is extravagant, the United States are not. But the reason why American democracy is not extravagant is purely local to the United States. The conclusion therefore follows:—the *inherent* tendency of democracy (witness Britain and France) is towards extravagance. Next he turns to corruption. France is corrupt: the United States are terribly corrupt: Britain is not. This is due to a peculiar local virtue of the British: and hence the conclusion stands that the inherent tendency of democracy is to corruption. In fact, Lecky started his enquiry with an implicit and private conceptual scheme by which he had denominated certain factors as "local and temporary." In so far as good was ever associated with democracy he attributed this to his local and temporary factors; thereby triumphantly proving that whenever evil was found associated with democracy it was due to the common and permanent factor—i.e. to democracy itself.'

Further examples of the same type of error may be brought out. For instance, the idea that proportional representation can be successfully applied only in monarchies or in states with a tradition of referendum—that is, only where there is an extra-parliamentary force maintaining the stability of political life—

[1] W. E. H. Lecky: *Democracy and Liberty*, Longmans. Two Vols. 1899.

although the monarchical element may be almost without practical importance and although the system of majority election may have worked with equal success in states with a referendum. But errors of this description are by no means caused by the nature of things, but only by the human failing of wanting to draw conclusions on the basis of insufficient data, something which already Sherlock Holmes warned his friend Watson against and which is just as dangerous to political scientists as to would-be detectives.

Comparison in the present field can deal chiefly with two things, namely with *institutions* and with *functions*.

Institutional comparison is in a sense the easier of the two. We deal here with such phenomena as parliaments, monarchies, presidents, ministers of finance or of the interior, political parties, pressure groups, electoral procedure, etc. The number of examples is unlimited. Comparison in this case involves, first, relatively detailed description of the institution in question, and, second, an attempt to make it clear which details are similar and dissimilar, respectively. To take a simple example: the monarchy in each of two countries may prove to have approximately the same amount of historical traditions behind it, identical or similar rules of succession to the throne and the same constitutional powers; but in one of the two countries the constitutional powers are more fully used than in the other. As a rule a much greater number of points has to be covered, but they all are of roughly the same type.

This seems straightforward enough. But in going farther into the matter, we are immediately confronted by a number of difficulties. To begin with, and perhaps most important, superficial details are apt to be over-emphasized in comparison of this type. Much time and energy is spent on discussion of the niceties of electoral procedure, party organisation, etc., and there is considerable danger that the student begins to draw conclusions from these similarities or dissimilarities without sufficient analysis of their real importance in the context.

But there are other difficulties as well. Are we really dealing with the same institution simply because the name remains the same? Is monarchy in Saudi Arabia really comparable with monarchy in Denmark? Is an election the same thing in India as in the United States? Does parliamentary responsibility mean the same thing in France as in the United Kingdom? Actually, quite often so many details are different that we might be justified in saying that identity in name while not a mere coincidence is yet without basis in substance.

In making comparisons at the institutional level, we therefore have to take various characteristics into account. The genesis of the institution as well as of its specific characteristics require attention. Can one speak of a 'common ancestry' for the institutions in the countries concerned? What was the purpose in its creation, if any? Was the original purpose attained along the same lines in the different countries? And finally: what is the importance of the institution in the total political and social configuration of the country? When dealing with the last-mentioned problem, we have to consider the general character (*Gestalt*) both of the political environment and of the institution in question.

Having gone into comparison of this type we then may go farther and try to determine the causes (in terms of present needs) of important specific characteristics, whether similarities or differences. In doing so, however, we already begin to pass into a study of functions, and indeed comparatively little interest attaches to institutional comparison except as a basis for the study of functions.

On the other hand, *functional* comparison is much more complicated. This procedure, which has also been called 'dynamic comparison,' may be quite ambitious. Let us quote Professor Macridis: 'It is the study of processes and the actual performance of functions by various systems. Here we attempt not only to identify structures through which certain functions are performed but also *to account* for the structural variations between systems. It is at this stage that we attempt to do three very important things in comparative government: (*a*) *account* for a similarity in occurrences in the light of analogous conditioning factors, i.e. two-party system and majority electoral system; (*b*) *account* for differences in the light of different conditioning factors, i.e., multi-party system and a majority electoral system and ethnic minorities; and (c) *attempt to predict* future occurrences in the light of a chain of conditioning factors that we have identified. This last stage is indeed the most significant one but at the same time the most difficult to reach.' Again, the number of examples is almost unlimited: we may try to compare the actual working of elections, of the administrative process, the emergence of leading figures in political parties, the activities of pressure groups and their relation to legislators, the rule of the military initial life; or we may be ambitious enough to attempt an over-all comparison of the whole working of the governmental process.

Here again, we are confronted with the problems of purpose (apparent or real) and result. But even if we should find almost complete similarity in both result and purpose, our work has not yet reached the end. There may be differences at the intermediate stages and, indeed, the quest for such differences may alone give value to the study. For instance, in Britain and in the United States the purposes of local government may be roughly the same, and in units of the same type we may find that they are attained to approximately the same extent. Yet the whole procedure of government is different, and the differences in the choice of means to attain the same purposes are exactly what we are trying to study.

There is a theoretical problem of the first magnitude involved in such investigations. They provide the one possible means of determining whether we can begin to speak of a 'common political process' as between different countries. For the future elucidation of this theoretical problem, it is useful to apply the techniques mentioned earlier in this section and try to determine whether we can speak of any 'common political process' as between different institutions in the same country. For instance: how do the decision-making processes compare in the House of Commons, in the Labour Party, and in the Trades Union Congress? If we find a considerable amount of consistency at this level, we still know nothing as to the similarity as between different countries, let us say Great Britain and the United States. If, on the other hand, we should find very great differences, it *may* still be true that the process in the House of Commons is similar to that of the House of Representatives and the process in the T.U.C. to that of the A.F. of L. and C.I.O.; but in view of the importance of cultural environments the balance of probability certainly seems to be against it.

The problem of *'comparability versus uniqueness'* has been brought into the discussion; and the question has been put whether each country and indeed each phenomenon in the given country is not unique, thus making comparison impossible. There seems, however, to be little need for serious consideration of this point. The problem applies to all descriptive classification, as Professor Sartori pointed out very forcibly in a paper to the Florence conference. As already emphasised, comparison always involves abstraction: we leave consciously out of consideration a number of characteristics and base our typology exclusively on those which remain. This would be unrealistic were we to claim that phenomena considered as belonging to the same 'type' were virtually identical, but as long as we are conscious of the fact that our typology is a mere abstraction it may be helpful to our understanding of each of the phenomena, as well as of the *Gestalt* which we are studying. Party patterns are 'unique' in every country, yet nobody in his senses would declare that it is impossible to compare, let us say, the influence on parties of the Roman Catholic Church in France, Italy and Western Germany. What we have to do in making such comparisons is always to keep the context in mind. In spite of differences in 'setting,' we find certain similarities; in spite of a general 'pattern' we find national variations. It is immaterial which of the two approaches we use, for the problem remains the same in both cases, and both methods correctly applied will lead to the same conclusions.

All these reservations, however, bring us back to the question whether the results we can hope to attain by comparison in the political field are really worth while. It all depends on the point of view. We are dealing with causes; but we must never imagine that causality means the same thing here as in the exact mechanical sciences. Even where, by exception, we may find something resembling mathematical correlation, there is always the possibility or even the probability of unknown variables. If nothing but exact results can satisfy us, then we may just as well discontinue our efforts. If, on the other hand, we are humble enough to be satisfied with approximations, and if we are able always to keep in mind that they *are* approximations, then our comparisons may still prove of interest.

This is important particularly when we return to the question of what we hope to attain by comparative studies. Is the purpose the establishment of a general theory? Is it even logically possible to build up anything of that sort? Is it possible now or in the near future? Can we hope to find even the main elements of a 'common political process' covering all political situations in all countries and in all fields? Practically speaking, such a contingency certainly seems a long way off. Logically speaking, we are confronted with a general problem of validity which therefore is particularly important for the methodology of comparative studies as contrasted with the description of 'unique' phenomena.

However, there are compensations. Whatever the difficulties and whatever the limitations hardly anybody would deny that we are building up *parts* of a theory in the form of partial problem solutions at least limiting the number of alternative possibilities. And in the last resort comparison, however inconclusive, helps us to refine our instruments of description and to understand each particular case better as we are comparing it with others.

PART TWO

THE APPLICATION OF COMPARATIVE METHODS IN POLITICAL SCIENCE

INTRODUCTION

IT has been repeatedly pointed out that it is only in the application to definite problems that the principles and problems of comparative government can be properly evaluated. Thus, to a large extent this evaluation must be left to those scholars who produce such monographs. What we can do here, largely on the basis of past achievements by a number of scholars and over considerable periods of time, is on the whole nothing more than to remind the reader of the numerous and various questions which can be posed in the course of this procedure. Even the list of questions can never become anything like complete, since not only answers but even questions frequently develop out of the materials which we are studying; but there may be some value in a comparatively full selection of examples from different fields, and in any case it will soon be obvious that there is an *embarras de richesse* of interesting topics which can be investigated only by the use of a comparative, as distinct from an atomistic approach.

AREA STUDIES—AN EXAMPLE OF THE CONFIGURATIVE APPROACH

IT was in the United States that the term 'area studies' first became popular. Originally, they appeared as a teaching programme, taking the form of a group of courses given in a university and devoted to various aspects of a given country or group of countries. The meaning was at first not very clear: it seemed that nothing beyond geographical contiguity was involved. And indeed, the idea of 'area' institutions is still only a very provisional concept. A number of problems remain unsolved with regard to the choice and delimitation of areas to be studied—but, more important, also in the actual use of the area approach, whether for teaching or for research. It is the latter type of problem which we shall attempt to discuss here.

Recently, a general criticism has been levelled against area studies as lacking in 'clarity and consistency.' It has been argued that 'the concept of an area is . . . operationally meaningful for purposes of comparison' only if it corresponds 'to some uniform political pattern against which differences may be studied comparatively and explained.' The idea of using geographical, historical or cultural definitions of the areas to be studied by political scientists is thereby rejected.

It is submitted that a criticism of this type, as it stands, is manifestly unreasonable. It is true that there has often been a considerable amount of abuse and a lamentable lack of clarity in using the area concept. But how should we know about 'uniform political patterns' until we have made our comparisons in the form of area studies? Moreover, it should be remembered that the idea of an area is only an auxiliary concept. In one sense, no definite areas exist, since not only 'political patterns' but also all other social and cultural patterns are eternally both similar and dissimilar wherever we go. In fact, it is not seriously important if the delimitation of the area in question proves a little dubious. We are only dealing with one approach to comparison. Also, the same country may very well be included in different areas. India, e.g., may be studied together with Pakistan and Ceylon, but it may also be linked with China. Pakistan, in turn, may be linked with India and Ceylon; or with other Moslem countries in Asia; Ceylon with India and Pakistan, but possibly also with Indonesia. Similar examples could be quoted to an almost unlimited extent. On the other hand, there are undoubtedly certain practical considerations to be considered, such as the drawbacks which seem to follow from choosing very large areas, so as to try, for instance, to divide Asia into the two parts of the Middle East and the Far East. If the areas chosen are more limited in size and scope, diversification within the area is almost automatically reduced and this very definitely simplifies our procedure.

In determining the areas to be studied, much is, in fact, to be said for an approach quite contrary to that of the critics just quoted. Probably both the easiest and the most fruitful method is to choose a criterion *outside* the realm of political science and to examine to what extent 'uniform *political* patterns' can be found where the existence of uniform geographical, historical, economic, cultural or other pattern has already been established. This may mean that we simply start from geographical concepts and study the similarities and dissimilarities of contiguous countries; but on the whole historical development, economic structures and social patterns, in so far as they can be established, seem to present the best bases for our choice. More important than geographic contiguity, is for instance, whether the countries studied have the same or similar religions— Protestant, Moslem, etc., 'areas'—or whether they have for some time formed part of the same political unit. Thus, the word 'area' is, in fact, not very appropriate. We shall continue to use it here, but with the reservation that area terms such as that of 'the Middle East,' 'the Far East,' 'the Northern countries,' etc., are meaningful only if it is understood that the main basis of the concept is not to be found in the geographical field but rather in general historical and cultural development and structure.

The critics just quoted also made a strong diatribe against what they called 'parochialism.' It is difficult not to agree with them at this point. When they say that 'the study of comparative government has been primarily parochial in its emphasis upon Western systems,' they are speaking no more than the truth. There are a number of perfectly good explanations and excuses, but on the whole it is true that only a limited number of countries have been studied, and equally true that it is necessary to go farther and include new areas. 'New areas,' it might be submitted, however, can be defined only as areas not previously studied. It is not certain that those areas necessarily have anything in common beyond the 'novelty' of not having been studied before. In principle, that would be correct. But in fact, the areas and countries which have been the object of study are primarily those belonging to Western Europe, the United States and the British Commonwealth; and consequently there is considerable reason to believe that we shall be able to find at least one more characteristic common to most of those who have been formerly left out. The majority of such regions fall under the conventional heading of 'underdeveloped' countries. In choosing its fields of study, political science has tended to take those which were by Western standards 'interesting,' that is, relatively highly developed. This should not be taken to mean that *all* highly developed countries have been the object of comparative study. But on the whole, when we speak of 'new' areas to be studied, we think chiefly of Asiatic, African and South American regions. To study these is important not only on general principles but also because of what we can learn about the validity of our criteria and the specific characteristics of the West in extending our studies to these 'new' areas.

In any case, whether areas are 'new' or 'old,' it can hardly be denied that area studies give the problems of comparative government in a nutshell. In the first place, the configurative approach is indispensable; and in the second place, the number of variables, while frequently still very large, is at least reduced in the case of a happy choice of area. Consequently, while area studies are of the very essence of comparative government, they also are more manageable than studies of an institution covering, or attempting to cover, the whole field.

What problems should be introduced into an area study? We may begin with some general observations. As usual when attempting synthesis, we have to take stock of *what* we know, as well as of what we do *not* know and of *how* we know the things which have come within our knowledge. In the case of comparative studies, this is particularly important. Comparison, furthermore, must take place both between different countries, etc., *within* the area to be studied, and *between* that area and others of which some knowledge has previously been acquired.

Secondly, we begin as usual with the 'superficial,' descriptive approach. Then follows the need for explanation, which in turn gives more depth to the study. We try to ascertain the mechanics of politics (whether or not they are democratic politics); the legislative procedure; the administrative structure; existing forms of self-government; etc. The next step is to investigate parties and other organised groups, as much as other forces behind the mechanism: social, cultural and economic. And that, finally, leads us to an inter-disciplinary approach.

A number of fundamental concepts and problems are involved in our study. Individual area studies cannot give an answer to all these questions. On the other hand, the answers are subject to influence from the general concepts of the student. The result of a study is always to some extent determined by the subjective attitude of the researcher in such respects, but area studies illustrate some of the difficulties of this type with special clarity.

To give an example: it is asked whether we can speak of a 'unity of human society.' Some authors assume that we can, others hold opposite views, and undoubtedly area studies organised on one or the other assumption will be to some extent different in character. But in any case, whatever the original attitude of the student, the study itself will contribute to the establishment of an attitude in this respect on the part of whoever follows it.

A similar general question is whether we are primarily interested in similarities or in differences. Obviously, both are important. But if we assume similarity, regarding difference as the exception, this will create an approach rather different from the one found if we assume uniqueness and regard every fundamental similarity as a fact requiring special explanation. Quite obviously, this question is closely connected with the preceding one, that of the 'unity of human society.'

Another general problem which will also come up is that of what might be called 'area consciousness.' It is a fact that people in the Scandinavian countries think of themselves not only as Swedes, Danes or Norwegians, but also as Scandinavians; and that Turks, Syrians, Iraqis, Egyptians and Israelis are conscious of the concept of the Middle East. Do attitudes of this type play any important part in the actual development of the countries concerned?

While it is necessary to include 'new' areas in our study, the 'old' ones remain important enough, especially for the development of our methodology. Lord Bryce's study of *Modern Democracies*, while definitely 'parochial' and partly very unsatisfactory for the student of the 1950's, yet remains a model in many respects. And especially it has set a pattern and coloured our attitude to such an extent that we are rarely quite able to liberate ourselves from it. With regard to the type of problems being involved in our comparison, it also provides a reminder of some of the minimum requirements necessary for the sort of thing we might attempt to do ourselves. On the other hand, there are few other books of the type and in particular of the level of Bryce's work.

An enumeration of some areas which could be studied on a comparative basis shows how far we have fallen short of satisfactory results even in the case of 'old' areas. We may begin as close to home as we like, and almost regardless of what is our home. There has been very much written about state government in the United States, but we are still lacking a proper comparative study of American state constitutions in theory and practice, whether on a historical or on a regional basis. The comparative approach is even more frequently lacking in the case of American municipal government.

Similarly proper comparative studies are largely missing in the case of the Western European continent which might be studied as a whole or divided up into a number of areas. To mention some examples of such areas, we have those of France and Belgium, that of the Benelux states, that of Germany and Austria, that of Scandinavia and Finland, that of Spain, Portugal and Italy. The dominions within the British Commonwealth have been studied by several authors, and the comparative approach has not been altogether lacking. Still, much remains to be done, especially in view of the rather rapid and partly unexpected development which has taken place after World War II. Another interesting area is provided by the 'satellite states' in Europe, i.e. by the non-Russian 'popular democracies.' A comparison between them, and perhaps in particular a comparison between a number of such states on one hand and the Soviet Union and its component republics on the other, would undoubtedly be illuminating. The problem, as so often, lies in the difficulty of finding a sufficient quantity of reliable and enlightening facts. And, finally, we need not limit ourselves to contemporary political and constitutional life. If we go back only as far as to the time between the two wars, there are at least two most interesting areas to be studied: the 'Baltic states' whose political development should probably be studied in conjunction with that of Finland; and other states created by the Versailles treaty, such as Poland and Czechoslovakia.

It appears already from this very brief survey that the possibilities of developing area comparisons are almost unlimited even with regard to the 'old' areas. Much remains to be done even if we maintain the 'parochial' attitude. Also, it should be remembered that a typology is indispensable to the establishment of comparisons between 'old' and 'new' areas. And such a typology may be more easily developed with reference to countries which have already been the object of study, although not always of *comparative* study. There are certain fundamental concepts which have already been established with regard to the Western countries. It remains to be seen whether they can be utilised for comparative purposes, and in particular whether they can be utilised for comparative purposes outside the areas for which they have originally been established.

But comparison within the 'old' areas is obviously not enough. The concepts may be developed there, but we cannot be quite sure of their applicability until we have gone beyond the 'parochial' field. Passing to the 'new' areas, it can hardly be denied that there are certain salient points which require more emphasis there than in the case of Western countries. Whether or not we adhere to the principle of the 'unity of human society,' at least in the initial stages we have to be aware of the fact that our concepts are largely based on the circumstances of the West and that we must therefore exercise particular care when passing beyond that orbit.

In the first place, as was pointed out by Professor Braibanti, the 'total fabric of society' is particularly important with regard to the study of Asia or other regions of a similar cultural structure. Thus, the problems of politics cannot be isolated even to the limited extent possible in the case of Western studies. Political instability is a more serious problem than in the West. Frequently political institutions have been created overnight; also, states themselves may be only in the process of emerging. Under such circumstances, the durability of the state itself and of its basic institutions is a fundamental problem. The maintenance of government (of *any* sort of government) may prove more important than the political structure. (On the other hand, it could be argued that the doubtful durability of states is a reason for an area approach to political studies; the alternative is to study states individually, and this may have its disadvantages if the states themselves are not sufficiently permanent.)

Now the importance of maintaining government, as opposed to that of establishing or maintaining a particular political system, also emphasises the role of nationalism. We should remember that in these circumstances nationalism is a means of integration, an attempt to widen the attitudes of the population from the traditional, very limited and—in the literal sense of the word—parochial approach to a concern with the nation as a whole. Consequently, the relationship between state and society is not the same as in more securely established states. It should be noted that this Hegelian distinction developed in the West in a period when corporativism was in the ascendancy, and that it is obviously of equal importance wherever there is an organised society offering an alternative to the organisation of the state—whether in the form of villages, of tribes or of organised religious or similar groups.

Furthermore, the politically conscious elements are frequently a small minority of Westernised and individualised persons. They are the forces who oppose the traditional influence of other social units, including those of family and clan, attempting to establish their own position and the position of a political entity at the same time and by the same means. This minority attempts to establish what might be called a common national ethos. For as a whole, the attitudes of the people of such regions as the Far or Middle East have originally been determined not by nationalism but by other larger or more limited loyalties, to religion—which includes a number of nations—or to the clan—which is only one of many similar units within the state. When areas of this type appear to be 'under-developed' by comparison with Western standards it is not only for economic reasons, but also because the actual structure of the state is so different. And the word 'under-development' is perhaps not altogether unwarranted. There was a time when the Western states were facing exactly the same problem, and this is also the reason why studies of this type could not be based exclusively on an investigation of contemporary circumstances but must include also historical studies.

Just as in the West during the Middle Ages, there are under those circumstances important psychological barriers to political activity, especially since such activity threatens to dissolve traditional loyalties. Only the Westernised, individualised *élite* willingly takes the risk of substituting new loyalties for the old ones. For this reason, this *élite* requires particular attention and has to be studied as it were separately from the majority of the population. This obviously does not mean that the majority of the population is not important but only that *élite* and majority both require equal and separate consideration.

As they stand, political institutions in 'new' areas are often recently established and sometimes copied from some Western model. This applies not only to the constitutional structure, parliamentary procedure, etc., but largely also to ideologies, including that of nationalism, which is frequently (as in India) taken over from the West in order to widen allegiances and form the basis of a state in the modern and in the Western sense.

With the relaxation of traditional ties political interest grows, in many different respects. Psychological barriers to political activity are overcome, first by the Westernised *élite* which is active on a higher level, later on possibly (again India seems to be the most interesting example) by larger and larger strata of the population. However, this further development may fail, whether because those larger strata of the population are unwilling to go beyond their traditional loyalties, or because the governing *élite* is not willing to take the risk of competition from other social groups.

In approaching these problems, it is argued that we must avoid the 'Kiplingian' touch. This means two things. In the first place, the idea of the 'white man's burden,' that is the self-evident superiority of Westerners, is today completely discredited, at least on the face of it. But on the other hand, Kipling's idea that 'East is East and West is West, and never the twain shall meet' is equally rejected. In any case, it must never be taken for granted. It is far from impossible that East and West have much more in common, psychologically, than Kipling was willing to assume, and that they will indeed be able to develop similar if not necessarily identical political institutions.

However, since we have not yet developed studies to the extent of being able to draw general conclusions, it is equally important not to take for granted certain Western categories, such as that of 'democracy.' This category may or may not be applicable. In fact this is one of the things to be established by comparative research, and until established it must remain an open question. It is true that many mistakes have been committed by those who assume that Western categories *cannot* be used in other settings; some of them undoubtedly have a universal application. But this discovery, important as it is, must not lead us to the conclusion that we can assume similar or even identical basic conditions everywhere. The idea of the 'unity of human society' has at most limited validity, and it is by no means certain that political institutions such as that of popular government are the same all over the earth.

It has also been argued that comparison is possible only as to compatible stages of evolution. Granting the idea of the 'unity of human society' this means that we are at present comparing societies at different stages of evolution; and this would apply both inside and between areas. For this reason, historical studies are indispensable in the field of comparative government. They may provide new points of comparison; e.g. the political problems of some 'under-developed' areas today may be more similar to those of France in the sixteenth or eighteenth centuries than to the Fourth Republic.

Native scholarship is undoubtedly indispensable for the development of studies of the 'new' areas. But it will prove useful only in so far as it does not provide us with 'parochialism' in a new and even more dangerous sense. Interest in non-Western areas must not be exclusive. To ignore the traditional objects of study, such as those of the West, would be highly dangerous, not only because these parts of the earth are after all comparatively important, but principally because they have provided us with the categories which we are attempting to use, and those categories are intelligible only to those who are familiar with the countries for which they were developed. Thus, while it is no doubt highly unfortunate if our studies are limited *only* to Western countries, yet such studies are at least still quite meaningful. But to apply Western categories to studies exclusively directed to non-Western conditions might well prove impossible and will in any case make deeper investigation far more difficult than a study involving both the Western and the 'new' areas.

Leaving these general observations aside, we also find that a number of special problems appear in the case of the 'new' areas. They are largely concerned with the 'depth' of our investigation and with the social structure in general. Obviously, whatever the type of area, we have to take into account such things as the occupational pattern, the extent of urbanisation, etc. Also, in the case of an area such as that of the Middle East, we must not forget that its semi-desert, semi-nomad character probably has important political consequences appearing not only in the actual political structure and in the character of social groups, but also in ideology, especially the religious ideology. Furthermore, under the circumstances of most 'new' areas one is bound to ask the question: what is the proper, or rather the natural sphere of politics? It is not necessarily the same as in the West. It may be wider—including units not regarded as political under Western circumstances—or more narrow, leaving aside some of the units which we study under Western conditions.

Taking existing entities into account we almost invariably find what might be called a pre-individualist collectivism. During the deliberations in Florence the question was asked whether it would not be possible to go directly from pre-individualist to post-individualist collectivism, by-passing the individualist period. An answer to this question is impossible without further study, and such a study must concentrate particularly on the circumstances of Communist society. For in many of the Communist countries an attempt has been made precisely to pass from one type of collectivism to another without passing through the individualist period. Actually, an object of much controversy within the Communist doctrine has been whether or not such development is possible; but on the whole opinion there seems to be in favour of direct transition. Is this only because such transition seems to be politically expedient, or is the assumption actually warranted by political experience?

The most important entity in 'under-developed' areas is usually the village. One, then, has to ask the question: is the village a part of political society or not? How far do primitive democracies form a basis on which a modern democratic society can be built? Or, to put the question differently, to what extent can primitive local democracy survive the establishment of an efficient national government?

Rather obviously, in a traditionally static society only certain limited groups are in favour of social change. The development of democracy is generally not the result of any particular desire for political power on the part of broad strata of the population, but rather a demand put forward by an *élite*. This applies not only to the 'new' areas: it has been equally true all over the Western world. The French revolution was actually, as we all know, the result of initiatives by a small but spirited minority; democratisation in England came through the Whigs in the early nineteenth century and the Liberals in the latter part of the same century; and National Liberalism in Germany was very definitely a movement of the upper middle class. In yet other cases, such as that of post-war Japan, democratisation has come directly from above. It was the Mikado himself who, on the advice of or under pressure from American advisers, took the initiative for the establishment of a democratic system of government. This, again, is not entirely without its counterparts in earlier Western history. There were what was called the octroyed constitutions in Germany in the nineteenth century, which, while not exactly democratic, yet meant a definite step forward in the Liberal direction. And the constitutional development of Denmark in the first half of the nineteenth century gives examples of a similar trend of development.

However, a constitution which is established on the wish of a small minority or on the initiative of a monarch is always in a rather precarious position. Actually, there are several examples of a governing group attempting to create real parliamentary government. Both in Turkey and in Puerto Rico the Government made the first attempts to establish an opposition. On the other hand, if such attempts are too successful and if the opposition becomes inconvenient the government which created it—or, perhaps, another government—may want to destroy it again and may easily be able to do so.

Another interesting fact is that the military has frequently acted as an instrument of development. Both in Japan round the turn of the century, in South America and in the Middle East, military groups have frequently been among the most advanced not only from a technological but also from the constitutional point of view. It would be a mistake to assume that officers as a group are always in favour of autocratic government, for again Europe of the eighteenth century provides certain parallels to what we see in the 'new' countries today.

What has been said here should not be understood to mean that 'democracy' in the 'new' countries is always something artificial and, as it were, synthetic. All that has been said is that an attempt to establish democracy in the Western sense generally comes from above, and that it may fail because of lack of interest on the part of the broader strata of the population. On the other hand it may also succeed. It is generally stated that India provides an excellent example of the success of a democratic system. Observers maintain that the Indian peasant is taking a genuine interest not so much in local affairs and other problems having a direct importance for him personally, but particularly in the larger issues of national or even international politics. Whatever the cause of the phenomenon, it very definitely shows that the creators of democracy actually succeeded in establishing an interest in the great problems of politics on the part of the numerically largest element in the population. Where this is the case, democracy seems to be relatively secure; it could probably be disestablished only with considerable difficulty and in fundamentally revolutionary circumstances.

In building up our area study, we shall undoubtedly find it possible and probably also convenient to approach it from the conventional starting point of 'political institutions.' Many examples can be given of fruitful problems in this field. We may study federalism in Latin America, in India and in Pakistan. We shall probably find that it means very different things in different countries, but also that it is an important factor in giving the respective states their particular character. On the other hand we shall also find that there are other territories, such as Iran and Turkey, where federalism could on the face of it well have been developed but where this has not been the case, generally for quite definite political reasons. Parliamentary structure, electoral systems, etc., provide an important field of comparison, although one in which special caution is required. We may study the structure of the executive power. We find monarchy in a number of countries, in the Middle East, in Japan, etc., and indeed monarchy with very real and tangible power. We find presidential government in Turkey and in the South American republics, sometimes with the President as head of the state and head of the government at the same time, sometimes with a President acting through a Prime Minister. We find parliamentary government in India, in Pakistan, and in the various Middle Eastern states, sometimes with a stable and sometimes with an unstable government. We find a number of dictatorships, and further study reveals that there are great differences between them. Dictatorship in Latin America does not necessarily mean the same type of absolute and powerful government as in Italy and Germany under the Fascist and Nazi regimes. Another study is that of public administration. Different countries have adopted different administrative models, and their choice has on the whole been made regardless of the basic political structures. Frequently, the bureaucracy has proved permanent even under far-going changes in the balance of power and in the constitution itself. Finally, we may find peculiar characteristics applying to specific institutions: for instance, the standing committees in parliament may either prove instruments of government influence over parliament— as in Japan—or provide parliamentarians with a direct channel to influence over the actual working of government—as in

Turkey. An observation of this kind can well be pursued over the area in question: what is the role of standing committees in the parliaments of the countries in the area? Do they have the same or different effects on the relationship between government and parliament in all states of the area? Can we find any particular explanation of the effect which the committee system has in the area we are studying, as compared to its result elsewhere?

A problem which is also conventional but yet leads us somewhat farther is that of the basis and character of political parties. What parties are there? How permanent are they? What is their ideological basis? What is their social basis? Can they be regarded as artificial creations, copied from the ideal or organised under Western influence, or do they express definite wishes and ambitions on the part of the population itself?

The character of popular influence, of course, requires special attention. Let us begin with civil rights: do they exist in theory; and if so, are they really safeguarded in practice? The means of safeguarding them are also of interest not only to the lawyer but also to the political scientist. This leads us to the next question. What are the political aspirations of the people? Are there any special aims which the broad strata of the population want to realise? In order to find answers to these questions, we must above all study elections. And there we are confronted with a problem which does not appear in the case of the 'old' areas, namely that of the effect of illiteracy on elections. One would assume, starting from Western experiences, that real democratic election is almost impossible under circumstances of illiteracy. On the other hand the reverse is confidently asserted. An answer to the question can be provided only by far-going and candid election studies.

A similar approach goes through the field of local self-government. How far does such self-government give expression to a real wish of the local population to accept responsibility in local affairs? Sometimes, one would assume, local government should provide an easier outlet for the political ambitions of 'under-developed' populations than national politics, but it is by no means certain that such an assumption is borne out by actual experience. Again, only descriptive studies of what happens in local self-government can give a reasonably certain answer.

At these points, more than in the field of political 'institutions' of the traditional type, it is obviously necessary to go beyond appearances, and even more definitely necessary to go beyond the confident assertions of those who find it in their interest to maintain one standpoint or another. 'Depth' is indispensable if we are to approach problems of this type.

But it is even more indispensable in other respects. What are the techniques of political leadership? Who becomes a leader? And by what means does he exercise his influence? What is the procedure when one leader is substituted for another? In a number of countries—perhaps even in whole areas—assassination is almost a recognised instrument of political party and group warfare. How can we explain it? A similar question applies to corruption. There are several types of corruption: corruption on a small scale, taking the form of 'baksheesh' to be given to all sorts of functionaries, and major corruption, that is large-scale bribes or similar favours given to leading politicians by those with great economic influence. To what extent does corruption exist? Which of the two types is prevalent? And what are the causes of corruption: insufficient salaries for public officials? Bad recruitment? Excessive administrative power? Is it principally in the administration or in parliamentary life that we find corruption on a large scale? Problems of this type will obviously shock many students and are particularly unattractive from the point of view of native scholarship, but we should remember that parliamentary government in Great Britain developed under circumstances where it could well be said that corruption was one of the most fundamental principles of the constitution.

Obviously, we shall frequently find that the superficial structure is misleading. There may be any number of apparently interesting constitutional organs which in practice have no importance whatsoever. The existence and basis of a ruling oligarchy is definitely much more important than the niceties of constitution and organisation. For instance, we have to study the role of the army in such areas as South America and the Middle East, where it has traditionally—and regardless of changing constitutional conditions—played a most important part. It could well be said that any study of Egyptian, Brazilian, or perhaps particularly of Japanese politics where the armed forces were left out of the picture would give a wholly false idea of the real political circumstances.

In dealing with political institutions and functions in the 'new' areas, one of our fundamental problems is that the categories of political science taken from the Western communities of the nineteenth and twentieth centuries are not always easily applicable. Only deeper investigation puts them in their correct light, and it is quite possible that further investigation will show the need for new and additional categories. A number of basic factors in political life have been never studied in the West because they are taken for granted in the largely homogeneous societies of Western Europe and North America. Here we are confronting new problems, whether because the 'unity of human society' does not exist or because we are dealing with varying stages of development. In any case, the two concepts just used can only be regarded as relative. Human society may be a unity, but it is obviously not uniform, and development does not always go in the same direction. For this reason, a study which is based on an application of even the most refined categories of Western political science may, in the case of the 'new' areas, prove insufficient.

But if it is necessary to go beyond those categories, this does not mean that we can neglect them. We can get much farther than we have yet done even on the basis of more or less con-

ventional approaches. One problem to be investigated in the
new environments, for instance, is that connected with propaganda and political activity. Which are the mechanics of propaganda? They frequently take forms very different from those
in the West, partly (but not entirely) because of the prevalence
of illiteracy. The role of the Teheran bazaar in Iranian politics
is worthy of study by itself, but it can also probably be made the
basis of comparative investigations: do similar business centres
play a similar part in other more or less unstable countries of
the Middle East? And do they perhaps appear elsewhere as well?
The effects of illiteracy make themselves known in many
different fields: they influence election techniques and the
character of election campaigns, for in both cases it is necessary
to substitute something else for the written word, as applied in
Western environments. The effects on propaganda technique
may be positive in that the population is more hungry for
information and for discussion and therefore more willing to
listen to political argument than in the West. The effect may
also be negative, in that the population does not have sufficient
background knowledge to understand the argument. It may
finally be asked—and it sometimes is—whether the two sides
do not balance each other comparatively well, so that illiteracy
has more effect on propaganda techniques than on the actual
contents and effects of political arguments.

And this brings us to political ideologies. To what extent are
we dealing with political ideologies proper, such as Liberalism,
Conservatism, Socialism, Communism, etc.; and to what
extent with non-political ideologies such as religion with certain
political and social implications? Here again, the West may not
provide us with the best categories. In fact, the role of religion
in politics has not been investigated properly even in Western
Europe. It is always difficult to study because of the strong
feelings involved on both sides. But in addition, religion may
not necessarily mean the same thing everywhere. The importance of religion in political life must to some extent depend on

which religion is involved. In Latin America, as in the major part of Western Europe, the most important political influence in the field is that of the Roman Catholic Church. In the Middle East, it is Mohammedanism. In the Far East it is sometimes also Mohammedanism, but more often Buddhism or some other religion specific to regions, such as Shintoism in Japan. Now, all these religions obviously have their different approaches to political problems. When Mohammed defined the state as an 'area of peace,' it is easy to understand at least certain parts of his meaning: there must be peace within the state; peace is not a normal situation outside the state. Naturally, an approach of this type is entirely different from that of the Roman Catholic Church. On the other hand, it is well worthy of study whether a strong religious influence in politics, regardless of what religion is involved, does perhaps lead to certain particular characteristics of public life. Furthermore, religion frequently appears as an issue. In 'new' as in 'old' societies, there is today very frequently a tendency towards secularisation, and the consequences of such tendencies might be quite different in this type of society from what they have been, let us say, in France. In any case, they are closely involved in practically all aspects of political development.

In another case also, we may speak of a peculiar ideological trait. Imitation of the West appears as a conscious process in government. What is the ideological basis for such imitation? A genuine desire to swallow Western ideals whole, or only an attempt to use the external characteristics of Western civilisation in order to further deeper ideals coming from the country itself? Again, this may properly be studied on a regional basis, but if we consider two of the most well-known examples of such imitation, Japan and Turkey, we shall at least find some characteristics making it probable that imitation does not go particularly deep. This does not mean that its effects may not be important. Here again, quality and quantity both require attention.

To what extent are Western influences, superficial or fundamental, conscious or unconscious, determined as to their extent and conditioned as to their character by the method employed in introducing them? This, in fact, is the problem of colonialism. It was maintained formerly that only a colonial system of government could have the effect of giving to the 'under-developed' areas (although they were not called so at the time) a sufficient dose of Western civilisation to enable them ultimately to carry on on their own employing Western methods and techniques in all fields, including that of constitutional life and politics. It is now maintained that colonialism has created such hatred of the West that colonies, and perhaps even former colonies, are unwilling to accept Western ideals because they are associated in the minds of their peoples with the hated colonial rule. Surely, some investigation could be made as to which of the two assumptions comes closer to the truth in a given area—for there is no necessity to assume that the answer will be the same all over the world.

And this, finally, brings us to what is probably the most fundamental problem in the study of 'new' areas and in comparing them to the West. Are the differences between Western nations on the one hand and the recently developed independent political units on the other fundamental, unchangeable differences? Or are they perhaps differences of degree and differences of development, so that we shall find, by comparing the areas in question with Western areas at a convenient state of development, that the similarities far outweigh the differences? This, of course, is the most difficult problem of all; and it is also the type of problem where so strong sentiments are involved that no really valid answer can be expected. We should perhaps not even set out to seek for an answer to a question of this type, but we could hardly refrain from thinking of it, and indeed it is probably necessary to keep it in mind as an open question, so as to avoid unwarranted assumptions.

There is little more to add at this point: after all, methodology develops only in the actual conduct of study. We may agree on the general procedure: to begin with a 'superficial' approach, to carry on to find the need for explanation and 'depth' in our research, finding invariably that an interdisciplinary approach is necessary. We have pointed out a number of examples of problems, the importance of which is immediately apparent, while being conscious that we shall find many more problems as our research continues. What more can we do until we have actually got the investigations going?

A few final observations may be permissible. In the Florence discussions, some striking parallels were drawn between Middle Eastern and Far Eastern conditions. This might imply that the specific characteristics of 'new' areas are largely to be found in the fact that they have not passed through the same stages of development as the West, not in specific conditions caused by their cultural patterns and earlier history. But subsequent conclusions may be quite different, even if this is granted. It may be that these areas are bound to pass through the same stages of development as the West, even if perhaps a little quicker, and that they will then develop to more or less complete similarity to the Western states. But it is equally possible that their development will be different, and that, therefore, the categories and the characteristics which we have worked out on the basis of our Western experience will continually prove inapplicable. In other words, the similarity between different 'new' areas may lie exclusively in the fact that they are *not* similar to the West—i.e. the similarities may be wholly or almost wholly negative in character.

In making our comparisons both between and within areas, we should note that there may be good reasons to combine 'old' and 'new' areas which have something in common. Comparisons might be particularly interesting between Japan of today on one hand and on the other either nineteenth-century Germany or the present-day United States; similarly, India and Pakistan should be compared with the United

Kingdom, since so many of their institutions have been drawn from the erstwhile mother country; Indonesia should be compared with Holland, China with the U.S.S.R.

Another observation should be made, although it is on the whole of an entirely pragmatic nature. A great number of difficulties come through the defensive propagandist attitudes of the nations themselves and their governments. This is true everywhere, but it is probably more true in 'new' areas than in the more highly developed democratic countries of the West. Moreover, this difficulty becomes much greater and more serious in the case of native scholars than in the case of observers from the outside. For this reason, perhaps, we should be willing to give wider scope to investigations by outsiders in this case than would otherwise be normal.

INSTITUTIONAL AND FUNCTIONAL COMPARISON: GENERAL OBSERVATIONS

IN the case of area studies, we were dealing with the configurative approach. But this is not universally applicable unless political science is to degenerate into a Hegelian variety of 'Gestaltpsychologie.' We must be equally prepared to study specific problems of a general character. These problems are institutional or functional in character, or possibly both. There is a definite difference here: the institutional approach deals with the structure and working of a particular institution, such as the legislature, whereas the functional problem is concerned with the development of certain functions, for instance the methods of legislation. Very frequently the same problem appears under both aspects: the institution of the legislature can be understood only in its relationship to legislation; whereas the problem of legislation is very largely connected with the working and structure of the legislature. But there is no identity: the legislature may have more important functions than that of legislation, and part of the legislative process may take place within the framework of the executive.

Since we are not concerned with the configurative aspects, the object of our studies is rather more limited than in the case of the area approach. We are dealing with the state, not with society as a whole. The comparative study of society in general should obviously be left to the sociologists. On the other hand, ideas and ideologies must be considered, since they are frequently very closely connected with the functioning of political institutions and indeed with the establishment and choice of such institutions. Incidentally, we shall find that ideologies are sometimes international, sometimes national in character, and that a comparative study of political ideologies on the basis of national differences is perfectly possible and probably in many cases most useful.

It is quite clear that we must attempt to pose problems, and to do so on a comparative basis. But the identification of the problems—let us say, the problem of legislation—is not always altogether easy. To what extent is legislation really the same thing in different environments? Even if we stay within one country, considering different historical periods, we shall find that in Britain, to choose only one example, legislation in the sixteenth century was not at all the same thing as legislation today. It is not easy to say whether we are even entitled to speak of legislation in the modern sense when dealing with sixteenth-century Britain. And similarly, it may be doubtful whether the term legislation can be used with the same meaning in France and in Ethiopia. In any case, even if we decide that we are entitled to do so, we must immediately stop to consider what the conditioning factors are in each case— that is, what differences are making legislation in France so different from legislation in Ethiopia.

What criteria of relevance can we use in choosing our problems? Few questions can be more endlessly discussed than this. In a paper for the Florence conference, Professor Herman Finer stated that 'it seems that we need criteria of *three* kinds. (1) We need to know what is *political*. (2) We must grasp what *sociological* factors affect the political. (3) We need to know to what *depth* of search into the sociological factors to go to find an explanation. The first criterium of relevance is, what is government; what is a constitution?' At this point, we are primarily concerned with the first type of criteria, those relating to what is political. Further specification was attempted in a paper for the same conference by Professor Macridis:

(a) The function of politics (decision-making: recon- ciliation of conflict, adjustment).

(*b*) The organisation of political authority (types of organisation: decision-making: how decisions are made).

(*c*) The power relations in any system (the nature of *élites* and decision-makers other than the political *élites*; relation between political *élites* and other *élites*, the study of groups and group interaction).

(*d*) The social and economic organisation of the system with reference to the organisation of authority, the performance of services, the attainment of desired goals.

(*e*) Ideology and the value pattern of a society with reference to the organisation of political authority; the nature and function of *élites*; the prestige and status elements in any system; the existing role allocation in a society.

(*f*) The role and position of the individual (motivation patterns; satisfaction of wants; welfare).

On the basis of questions such as these, we then go on to choose our fields of research and comparison. To borrow again from Professor Herman Finer, some of these seem to be institutions; functions; the study of an operation of government; and the particular elements entering into government and in specific institutions and functions. 'For example, Public Administration in any country may be studied systematically (apart from a combination of the five above-mentioned approaches) through the elements: the purpose to be achieved and the ethos therefore necessary; planning; organisation, staffing, co-ordination; reporting; budgeting. This is only one of the ways in which the subject may be attempted. It has tremendous values for comparison and clarity. For example, the administrative systems of America, Britain, France and Italy could be compared under these heads—further analysed, of course, into the known subdivision of these main elements.'

Of course, there is an unlimited number of examples of such

problems. Some of them were discussed at the Florence meetings, and we shall return to them presently, but for various reasons it seems best to begin with some of the problems *not* discussed at those meetings.

First: the general character of the state. Largely because of pluralist criticism, the traditional definitions of the state are no longer in vogue. It has been found that the deductive definitions developed especially in German political theory are not really very useful for an inductive approach to political studies. On the other hand, even if we apply the deductive method here as elsewhere, it is obviously not incompatible with distinguishing some fundamental problems in the existence and structure of states themselves, if not of 'the State.'

We have seen earlier with what latitude 'a political body or situation' can be defined. According to the definitions used here, such a body or situation exists outside as well as inside the state. On the other hand, practically everything connected with states is of a political character. This compels us to some consideration of what is meant by the idea of 'national interest,' whether applied (as in some cases) chiefly to questions of international politics or, as by earlier authors, such as Meinecke and Beard, also inside the national sphere itself. What is the national interest; how is it determined; to what extent does it have objective existence; to what extent can its establishment be explained and determined from a subjective viewpoint? More directly, the character of states can be studied by the question of how government is maintained—by consent, by constraint or, more usually, by both? Why are decisions obeyed? This is a type of question which is very definitely connected with the fundamental structure of states. And it is probably best studied in the analysis of political instability rather than stability. It is only when we find why decisions are, in some cases, *not* obeyed that we begin to understand why states are generally able to maintain their ascendency.

This type of problem, and indeed many others, take on a

special importance when we are dealing with states in the process of emerging. Such states may be altogether new, entities not existing formerly, such as Pakistan, but they may also be former colonies gaining independence from a mother country formerly responsible, among other things, for the maintenance of law and order. Fundamental problems are particularly interesting in states of this type, since we can follow the establishment of a government under circumstances where the maintenance of obedience to decisions was formerly in the hands of an outside agency but has now been taken over by the new state itself. Another aspect of the problem appears when we study the durability of existing states, i.e. the extent to which they are able to maintain themselves against tendencies of disintegration into several units or of being integrated into other, perhaps larger and more powerful units. Obviously, this sort of problem applies not only to new 'democracies,' but to any state regardless of whether or not it is governed under a democratic system of government.

Passing to institutions, it seems convenient to begin with the traditional categories. First of all, we have the unitary or federal structure of the state. But federalism must be related to regionalism. We find this in the United States, where regional differences are undoubtedly very closely connected with the problems of federalism, as appears most clearly in connection with the relationship between the North and the South before, during and after the Civil War. Similar problems appear in the government of a number of Latin American states, although the solution may vary considerably from the North American pattern. On the other hand, regionalism may exist without federalism: there are a number of states, such as Turkey and Iran, where there are striking regional differences but no federal system of government. Moreover, the particularism of regions, whether or not expressed in federal form, may threaten the fabric of national government. But it may also be true in many cases that the state has not yet developed to the stage where even the smallest entities have begun to feel associated with the state as such, and in this case regionalism and federalism may well prove a means of integrating units which otherwise would never have been able to accept relationship to the nation as a whole.

Passing on to the general structure of government, we are, of course, immediately confronted with the problem of democracy. But it is important to make it quite clear what we are talking about. Democratic institutions may mean entirely or at least partly different things in recently developed democracies and in countries having already a strong and old democratic tradition. It should be emphasised that this observation applies not only to so-called 'under-developed' areas but also to countries in the West itself where democratic institutions have no basis in historical tradition and frequently not in national sentiment either. Even if we assume that democracy is an end in itself and should therefore be introduced everywhere as quickly as possible, we can never avoid the problems appearing because democracy is so strongly dependent on the environment, and perhaps first of all on the ideological environment. In Great Britain, Scandinavia and the United States democracy appears as a 'super-ideology,' accepted in principle by all conflicting groups and interests. In Germany and Turkey it remains on trial, and its final acceptance depends on its achievements.

But this is only part of the difficulty. More than any other category, that of political democracy is based on specific Western assumptions. It is largely influenced by Greek and Christian individualism and egalitarianism, and the democratic procedure of universal and equal suffrage in elections is a means of permitting consciously equal individuals to combine for the realisation of definite aims through the organs of their nation. The example, for instance, of Poland between 1919 and 1939 shows that this is a dubious concept where national feeling is not accepted and compromise is rejected; the latter was largely true even in the Weimar Republic. In any case, the tendency to put the emphasis on machinery rather than content—and political scientists have frequently sinned in this respect—is fatal whenever we are investigating democratic institutions in an unfamiliar setting. Frequent general elections and parliamentary procedures do not in themselves prove the existence of active popular influence in government; and it is this influence, rather than the technique by which it is achieved, which is the real meaning of political democracy.

Traditionally, we approach problems of popular government from the point of view of the constitutional structure. We have presidential government and division of power; we have parliamentary government, where the democratic system is applied through the close association of the executive and the legislative branch. Both can well be studied in their relationship to other particular institutions such as that of bicameralism, to the existence or non-existence of a power to dissolve Parliament, etc.

But any comparative political study should require us to go a little deeper than that and to investigate at least to some extent the varying forms of dictatorship and the varying circumstances in which dictatorship appears. Again, we must see to it that we are not misled by our natural sympathies. Even if we dislike dictatorship, even if we think that it is an evil which could and should be abolished everywhere, this should not lead us to imagine that dictatorship is always the same or to refrain from studying its different materialisations which are, at least, an indispensable study for anybody who wants to go a little farther into political demonology.

The central government is not the only object of our study. We have to deal with local institutions also. Here we find that the needs of modern society have led to reorientation of local self-government, closely related to the increasing pressure of work in local administration and the consequent new problems of function. There are similarities and dissimilarities in the way in which countries with long traditions of local self-government have been approaching this type of problem. And, obviously, again it is particularly necessary to keep the function of local self-government in mind when studying how it works in countries which do not have any such tradition.

Other administrative institutions must be studied with equal interest. There is the eternal problem of centralisation and decentralisation in national administration; and decentralisation may, in turn, be local or functional, or both. There is the question of how an administrative system (for instance that of France) works where it is transplanted to an entirely different environment (such as that of the Middle East).

Finally, we must not by-pass the judiciary, which should be studied not only in its relation to the general constitutional framework but perhaps more particularly in its relation to the legal system as a whole. Indeed, a much neglected group of problems is that of the political role of legal systems as such; for instance: to what extent has the Anglo-Saxon legal system influenced the development of the Anglo-Saxon political tradition?

Much interest has recently been given to the question of pressure groups in politics. They appear, indeed, in most countries today. But the problem must be widened. We must deal also with organisations outside the sphere of pressure groups proper, that is with groups which do not primarily exist in order to exercise political pressure, which may not even exercise such pressure consciously, but which in their relationship to the general structure are so important that they cannot help influencing political developments as well. Religious bodies are perhaps the best example of this. Also, the groups— whether pressure groups or not—are interesting not only because of the pressure which they exercise on political authorities in particular circumstances. We must also study their internal structure, including the existence of minor groups within the major interest groups. Also, we have to see what happens to small independent interest groups, representing small but active minorities, in the circumstances of different political systems and settings. Finally, we must take into account such groups as the military. What is the character of 'militarism'? It may be reactionary; but it has been pointed out that it may also be progressive. Here, comparisons may prove exceedingly useful. We have the traditional examples of Germany in 1870, in 1914 and in 1933, where the influence of the military was extremely important, regardless of what we think about the manner in which this influence was used. We have the experiences of Latin America; and we have the circumstances of the Middle East which have recently been made the object of a particular study.

A comparative approach to ideologies should perhaps be mentioned in this context, for ideologies are, of course, frequently related to special groups. But it is also almost a commonplace to speak of their importance in relation to institutions. The ideological basis of political institutions has frequently been discussed in the form of a spread of an institution on ideological grounds. The constitutions of the French revolution were copied in many other countries; the early twentieth century is characterised by the vogue of parliamentary government, influenced by British Liberalism; the 1920's and 1930's saw a spread of corporatism, obviously to be explained by the ideological influence of Fascist movements. Institutions can be understood only when we identify their ideological background. On the other hand, ideologies themselves may also be studied with comparative methods. There are national ideologies and international ones; and to the latter group belongs that of nationalism, which is indeed an international ideology, spreading to new territories and there creating an increasing interest both in political independence and in the maintenance of historical traditions. Even international ideologies adapt themselves to national environments and appear in very different forms in different circumstances.

Passing over to functions, the first problem is what functions are being fulfilled. We have to begin, of course, with the maintenance of law and order, the safeguarding of the existence of the state itself. This may take place by consent and by constraint, or, as has already been pointed out, usually by a combination of both. But their relative importance in each particular case could and should be studied.

Closely connected with this is the problem of justice. How is justice established? What are being regarded as the criteria of justice; and how are they attained? We shall frequently find that this leads us far beyond the concepts of eighteenth- and nineteenth-century European Liberalism. In modern circumstances, and indeed today in most parts of the world, we deal also with the idea of the 'welfare state' in the widest sense of the word. States, and not only prosperous ones, are assuming greater and greater responsibilities in the economic and social fields. It is part of our study to try to find out how this tendency develops, and in doing so we approach one of the most fundamental problems of all social sciences, the political consequences of industrialisation at different times and in different geographical environments. There is something of the 'Marxist' touch in this, since Marx and Engels already in the manifesto of 1848 pointed out to what extent political institutions are dependent on economic circumstances. However, whether or not this has anything to do with the materialistic concept of history, it is undoubtedly a proper problem for political scientists. And particularly in modern circumstances, this side of state functions is assuming wider and wider importance and frequently changing the very basis of the political structure.

But when the political scientist speaks of a functional approach, he thinks less of the development of a number of new functions than of functional procedure; that is, how institutions fulfil functions. Undoubtedly, such a combination of institutional and functional approaches is frequently the most useful one. And it has been used to a surprisingly small extent even in studies of the most developed single Western countries.

Let us take an example. We speak of legislation, and of the legislative procedure. To what extent are really comprehensive studies being made of the means by which a law, or a similar act comes into existence? We talk about the administration of justice and about civil rights. But we do not know very much about how they are actually established and maintained in different political systems. Here, we have every reason to compare systems and institutions of different types in relation to the functions they are attempting to fulfil. How are these problems solved in a federal and in a unitary system, respectively? How does totalitarianism work, and how does Liberalism work in this respect? What is the effect of division of power and what the effect of fusion of power with regard to these functions? Or we may approach the problem from the executive angle, investigating its bearing on decentralised and centralised administrative systems. A number of questions arise. We may have to go into the character of the *droit administratif.* We may study the constitutional role of the courts.

We may even have to investigate the problem of defence against outside attack, since the importance of such defence varies very much from one country to another. It is quite probable that the development of 'militarism' and the importance of the military in relation to the civil power is closely connected with the extent to which the country is threatened by attack from the outside. The study of the circumstances of the French revolution leads to this conclusion, and we probably come to the same result if we go to Latin America, to Germany, to France or to the Middle East, while comparing them with countries living in different circumstances, such as the United States, the United Kingdom and Scandinavia.

Inversely: how do institutions work? When speaking of the legislative process, we should do this not only in the terms of the procedure of the legislature, but in the widest sense, involving all stages from the first initiative taken in a newspaper article, up to the actual enactment of the law. Similar methods may be used in studying the procedure of the executive. In different forms of government we have cabinets, inner cabinets, etc. Where the chief of state is an actual power on or behind the accepted political scene, his relations to ministers become of paramount importance. But decisions are reached not only in the legislature and in the cabinet of the chief executive. How are administrative and judicial bodies able to reach a decision? We know the law in these matters, but we do not always know what happens in actual fact; and a full understanding of the administrative and judicial procedure is indeed possible only if we compare the actual circumstances in different environments. What is the actual working of local self-government? Again, we know the law; but we do not know the practice. The actual relationship of self-governing local bodies to central authorities differs very much in different administrative and political systems, and only a study with an intensely practical approach can give us a clear idea of what local self-government means in each case.

We may also employ a more unconventional approach. The role of corruption and the causes of corruption in different circumstances of the West and the 'new' areas is certainly worthy of study. The same is true of militarism—not that this is necessarily a form of corruption. The social and political causes of the influence of the military are equally important with the question of the permanence of bureaucracy in changing political fortunes.

Problems of this type are probably best approached on the basis of the concepts of power and leadership. Partly, but not wholly, those two terms actually mean the same thing; but leadership is at least supposed to mean power exercised with a greater amount of consent on the part of those to whom it is being applied. If we use this approach, we have perhaps in particular to go into the problems of political *élites*. We have to find out what is the *élite* in a given system, and what are the differences between *élites* in different systems. We have to study the social basis, the educational basis, the means of recruitment, and the means of renewal of the *élite*. We have to see whether the existing *élite* is dependent on a particular constitutional and political structure, or whether its existence may be maintained regardless of changes in institutions. We have to try to find out what techniques are being used by the *élite* in order to establish and maintain its ascendency. And we have to see whether the rule of the *élite* is being consciously accepted by the population as a whole, perhaps on ideological grounds, or whether it is rejected in principle although applied in practice.

The functional procedure is in many respects best followed and compared on the basis of case studies, illustrating the development of similar problems in different environments. The International Labour Organisation recommends a particular piece of legislation; what happens in different countries? We may try to find out how the law in question is being accepted, drafted and passed through parliament; but we must, of course, not stop there but also try to find out if and how the law is actually administered. Or we may look at police problems involving the maintenance of law and order in particularly different circumstances—there should be no difficulty in finding similar upheavals in countries which are otherwise different in character. On the whole, case studies of this type should not be too difficult to conduct, at least if we are approaching our work on the basis of a practical team spirit. Here is one of the cases where native scholarship can best be combined with international co-operation. If the leader of the team chooses a type of problem which is applicable in a number of countries, and if the native scholars present, with a minimum of comments, cases dealing with similar problems in their respective environments, the study of comparative government could gain more than anybody would imagine who is looking only to the limited range of the problem which can be studied by these means.

NATIONALISED INDUSTRIES

IT may seem surprising that we should take as our first major example one which is so far away from the traditional themes of political science, and indeed so specific, as that of nationalised industries (or, rather, public enterprises). On the other hand, it is methodologically a good example. It is relatively simple; there can be no doubt about the object of study, at least in the physical sense of the word. It is both institutional and functional in character, and it involves problems which are of intense practical importance in the circumstances of today. Thus, while in many senses relatively easy of approach, it involves an obvious need to consider both the institutional background, the institutional structure of the industries themselves, the character of the functions involved and also the ideological disputes attached to the problem of nationalisation. The difficulty lies particularly in the need for comparison with non-governmental economic enterprises, a comparison which is necessary for the assessment and evaluation of the public enterprises and which at least in some respects necessitates an interdisciplinary approach.

In studying the background it is necessary first of all to determine whether in that particular environment public enterprise is the rule or the exception. In modern Western society the economic structure has been built up on the basis of private enterprise, to be supplanted only partially by public inroads on the field. But outside the West this is not always the case. There are also environments where most enterprise is either nationalised, that is taken out of private hands and put under the direct control of public authorities, or created by the State itself. Quite obviously, other developments will vary in the two cases, although useful comparison can undoubtedly be made between the nature of public enterprises in a setting where they are the rule and one where they are the exception. From our point of view, it is probably most interesting to consider the case where public enterprise is the exception or, alternatively, where it was introduced on a large scale after a system of private enterprise had already been developed. On the other hand, it is necessary to consider other alternatives also, such as those of 'under-developed' areas where economic development is attempted almost exclusively by public organs.

Nor is the purpose of public enterprise always the same. Public ownership may apply chiefly to public utilities, either because those utilities have, to begin with, been developed by public action (as in Scandinavia) or because the experience of private enterprise in the field showed that it resulted in abuse of one type or another. Here we are already confronting an ideological problem. It may be argued that public utilities should be subject to public ownership regardless of efficiency, precisely because of their general character and because of the interest of all citizens in their management. It may also be argued that concessions to private enterprise would be equally acceptable in principle, but that practical experience has proved direct public ownership to be preferable. This type of problem becomes even more usual and even more serious in the case of services which may or may not be classified under the heading of public utilities, such as transport services. Here again, there is a difference between such transport services as are necessarily monopolistic or almost monopolistic (e.g. railways) and such which can be run on a purely competitive basis, such as highway transportation. Quite obviously, both the practical and the ideological argument would seem to apply more frequently in the case of the first than in that of the second type of transportation.

But of course public ownership may be much wider. We

have the case of public enterprise aiming at general economic development and kept in the hands of the state either because private capital is not willing to run the risk of initial losses, or because it is felt to be in the public interest to control costs and profits and prevent 'profiteering' which might be dangerous to the public good.

Another type of public enterprise is what has been called 'competitive public enterprise,' developed to establish competition in a field where a private monopoly is in existence or seems to be emerging. In this case, the public enterprise has the main aim of protecting the consumer and limiting the power of the private entrepreneur. It can, ideologically, easily be defended on grounds of the purest economic Liberalism. On the other hand, there may also be cases where a public enterprise of this type automatically becomes a monopoly itself, although a monopoly which, being controlled by the public, is regarded as a smaller danger to the consumer or, indeed, as being altogether in his favour.

There are many other types of public enterprise, such as the case where basic industries or other basic economic activities, often including banking, are put under more or less complete public control because of their particular importance. The argument may be the ideological one, that these economic activities are too important to remain in private hands; or it may be purely pragmatic, it being held necessary to keep them in public hands to guarantee sufficiently quick and strong development regardless of the immediate prospects of a good economic result. For the latter purpose in particular, public holding companies, such as the 'banks' in Turkey, are an interesting device. Similar cases arise with regard to new industries introduced into a country where private capital is not willing to run the risk. Or it may be a question of multi-purpose development, such as the Tennessee Valley Authority, where the public steps in because so many different private interests are involved or because the project is of such size that it is unlikely that a private capitalist will take it on. In fact, it is sometimes argued that banking is a multi-purpose activity of this type, and that public authorities may be wanting to step in here both to control the power of capital and to provide necessary capital for development.

At these points it is important to recognise the difference between the 'old' and the 'new' countries. In the former, industrialisation was achieved on the basis of private capital. It took considerable time and involved quite a number of social and other problems. In the latter, industrialisation is frequently being attempted at a much higher speed and it is desired to avoid the social evils which accompanied it in the older areas. On the other hand, the two groups are not entirely separate. Even in the 'old' countries, there are a number of examples of public enterprises such as the national railways in the Scandinavian states and in Germany, while in a number of 'new' countries private entrepreneurs, whether native or coming from the outside, are developing an economic power which is regarded by some observers as a menace.

We shall also, of course, have to deal with the circumstances accompanying the emergence of public enterprises. Are they an original feature of the economy of the country in question, or have they been established as the result of a conscious effort? In the former case, we may be interested to find out what was the reason for using public rather than private enterprise in the particular field. In the latter case, we are confronted with the reasons for nationalisation—ideological or other— with the methods employed, the political debate taking place at the time of nationalisation, the arguments advanced, etc.; and whether nationalisation took place more or less totally or by sectors, some parts of the economic life being left permanently or temporarily in the hands of private enterprise. One of the main interests here is to find out whether ideological or practical considerations were of primary importance.

Next, we approach the structure and form of public enterprises (nationalised industries). They may be public corporations, owned and managed more or less completely by public organs. They may be used to carry on economic activities directly or take the form of holding companies, controlling, in their turn, the action of other economic bodies. They may be mixed enterprises, organs that combine public and private ownership, and perhaps even public and private control. If the latter device is used—and it is indeed an interesting one—we have to ask whether the public or the private element predominates. Whatever form is used we further have to establish whether our public economic enterprises are national or local in character and whether they are part of an attempt to plan the economic system from the centre or, alternatively, an attempt to combine public ownership and decentralisation. Here again, both expediency and ideological considerations may come into the picture.

The internal structure and organisation of the enterprise is perhaps most obviously of interest to the political scientist. They may be direct government organs, such as departments of government, general directorates, etc.; local authorities, or the like; or they may appear superficially in the same forms as private enterprise, as limited liability companies or corporations. The latter form is frequently used in order to give to the public economic enterprise a greater amount of freedom than that generally allowed to a government organ. They may be controlled by the executive or more or less directly by the legislature. In the latter case, an interesting problem is whether control by the legislature is merely a matter of form or whether it is possible, regardless of party considerations, for members of the legislature to exercise direct influence on the working of the enterprises. If this is the case, we must further enquire how such power is exercised, particularly whether it is used to allow members to influence the enterprise in the interest of their particular constituencies.

The extent of autonomy allowed is, of course, of extreme

importance. Controls may be of different types. They may be direct and administrative; they may be financial in the sense that the budget of the enterprise has to be approved by parliament and by the executive; or they may be limited to control of investments or even to the contribution of new capital. An interesting method of control is that of the regulatory commission which, at least usually, is employed to control private enterprises but has the effect of giving the public such power over these enterprises that they may remain private in name rather than in substance.

The functioning of the enterprises must, of course, also be studied, not only in the technical sense of seeing how decisions are reached, etc., but also with regard to the policies pursued and the criteria of efficiency employed. Here we confront a methodological problem of some magnitude. Is it our function to try to establish whether and to what extent public enterprises are efficient, perhaps even in comparison with private enterprises of a similar type? The present writer would venture to submit that this is *not* the case. It is true that we can never study public enterprises without going at least to some extent into the field of economics; but the question to what extent these enterprises are efficient can surely not be regarded as one of political science. It is rather one of politics; even the economist may not easily reach definite conclusions in matters of this type. What interests the political scientist is thus not whether these enterprises are efficient but the methods employed to find out whether this is the case, and the criteria of efficiency actually employed. These are particularly important from the point of view of ideological study.

As to the practical approach, it is submitted that this is a field where case studies would be of particular interest. It should not be difficult to find comparable cases in different environments. For instance, we may investigate how the various national railway systems are organised and managed; or how a number of cities are managing their utilities. Comparison may be of interest, not only between different countries, but—in the field of local enterprises—also between regions of the same country. Moreover, this is also a field where comparison between more and less developed areas should probably be both possible and profitable.

PARLIAMENTARY PROCEDURE

IF nationalised industries are a comparatively novel and also limited field of study, parliamentary procedure is one of the traditional objects of the study of political science. Naturally; since it has been of basic importance in the development especially of the Western democracies and still remains very important to the working of their government. Also, while involving a great number of details, it presents comparatively few methodological difficulties. Our problems are almost entirely institutional, and it may well be said that we can as a rule stop at a comparatively 'superficial' approach. The difficulties lie in the mastering of many details and in the delimitation: which observations and questions are to be included in our study?

The procedure of any parliament depends, of course, on its general structure, its constitutional position and its function. To begin with structure, we have unicameral and bicameral legislatures, and of the latter type there are many different varieties. In this respect, it is probably especially important to know whether the two houses have exactly the same functions, or whether there are any important differences in that respect as between the House of Representatives and the Senate of the American Congress or, even more strikingly, between the two houses in the British Parliament. But constitutionally, the most important fact is the relationship to the executive. Are we dealing with a system of division of power or one of fusion of power—with a 'constitutional' or a 'parliamentary' system of government? Quite obviously, the answer to this question has important consequences for the character of parliamentary work, as we find by even the most superficial comparison of the American and the British legislatures.

Different functions require different procedures. Traditionally, the basic function of a legislature is to legislate. But legislation, in the sense of the actual passing of specific Acts, or laws, is not necessarily its most important function today. It depends not only on the constitutional structure but also on the general needs of society whether or not legislation takes up very much of the time of parliament. Taxation and budgeting are frequently (but not invariably) organised in the form of legislation, resulting for instance in a Finance Act; but even where that is the case, financial procedure generally differs very much from general legislative procedure. Many countries have developed a system of delegated legislation: the executive may have the right to legislate in certain fields and under certain conditions. Parliament may afterwards have a right or duty to pass on the admissibility of legislation already enacted in this form. Its action may take the form of passing legislation to take the place of the provisional Acts, of passing a general Act, approving the action taken by the executive; or other forms, such as that of resolutions, may be employed in this case. On the other hand, the terms of the enabling Act may be such as to dispense with any specific *ex post facto* controls. Finally, there is the question of control over the executive which, especially in countries with a parliamentary form of government, seems in many respects to be the most important function of parliament, and which may necessitate particular devices, such as questions, interpellations, etc.

Procedure itself involves a number of basic problems. If we have a bicameral system, procedure may be simultaneous—the two houses debate the same question at approximately the same time and reach their conclusions without knowledge of what has happened in 'another place.' More frequently it is consecutive: measures are passed first by one house and then by the other. In the latter case there may or may not be special rules as to which house should come first with regard to particular types of proposals such as the budget. Since the consecutive system is so much more usual than that of simultaneous consideration, it has also developed a greater number of variations.

What is the role of the Speaker? He may—as in the British House of Commons—be an entirely impartial officer, equally respected by all sides (or at least attempting to gain such respect) and charged chiefly with maintaining the orderly procedure of the assembly; or he may, as in the United States House of Representatives, be a party leader expected to use the rules of procedure for the benefit of his own party and charged with a number of functions which could not easily be held by an impartial umpire of the British type.

Probably the most important factor in a number of systems is the committee system. Committees, in the sense of more or less independent bodies acting as preparatory agents for the houses or for parliament as a whole, exist in most countries, but not everywhere—the procedure of the British House of Commons is based on the absence of committees of this type for most business, although standing committees are sometimes used to provide an alternative to debate in the house as a whole. Where committees exist, it may be the rule that all business under consideration should first pass through a committee stage; or there may be exceptions to this rule. Committees may be separate for each house or joint committees. Obviously, this is a question which is closely connected with that of consecutive or simultaneous procedure; in fact, simultaneous procedure can hardly be possible except under a system of joint committees. Finally, the relationship of committees between them is of interest. In some parliaments, such as that of Finland, one committee is superior to all the others; in a number of other systems, also, the same matter may be referred to one committee after another. But in most countries a matter can be referred to only one committee, which assumes responsibility for reporting on all its various aspects.

Who sits on committees? Are there representatives of all groups in parliament; and to what extent does the majority maintain effective control not only over the decisions but over the procedure of committees? Do members of the Government sit on committtees or appear in some other capacity during their debates; and, if they do, do they appear as leaders or as witnesses of the type known in the case of American committees?

The working procedure is of extreme importance. For instance, do the committees hold open or closed executive sessions? It seems to be an accepted principle of the Anglo-Saxon parliamentary system that committee meetings should, at least to a considerable extent, be open to the public, whereas in a number of other countries one of the greatest advantages of the committee system is seen in the fact that it provides an opportunity for political discussions undisturbed by the press. Again, this depends to some extent on what is the objective of the work of committees: to provide an opportunity for debates or to attempt to reach a practical solution. It depends also to some extent on whether the committees are large or small in membership, and whether they work in plenary sessions or are divided up into sub-committees. Another aspect of the committee system is concerned with hearings. As a rule committees will need an opportunity to call in outside experts, but this may be done in different forms and either allow the experts to be mercilessly cross-examined by the committee or use them simply as a means of finding out the facts necessary for reaching a reasonable conclusion. Finally, there is the question of the relationship between the committees and the Government. In some cases, especially standing committees where members sit for one legislative period after another may be means of exercising very strong control of the Government; but cases have also been cited—such as that of Japan—where the Government is able to exercise stronger pressure over committees than over the general sessions of parliament.

Parliamentary procedure, of course, also involves the forms of debate on the floor of the house. And debating procedure in parliament is especially interesting since it generally provides a model on which all public meetings in the country are managed. Systems for making and amending motions differ almost to an unlimited extent between different countries. Rules of debate are also very different, both with regard to the order in which speakers are allowed to appear and the possibilities of curtailing the debate, either by limiting the time of each speaker or simply by closing the debate before all who desire to speak have had an opportunity to do so. Finally, there is the voting procedure, which is, of course, closely connected with the question of how motions and amendments are to be presented.

All these questions are important and interesting in themselves and provide a fertile field for comparison between different countries and types of countries. But it is submitted that no study of the rules of parliamentary procedure can become really elucidating if it is not correlated to the party system in parliament. Whether the party system is the result of the rules of parliamentary procedure, or whether the latter have been drawn up in accordance with the party system, the two are very closely intertwined, and, in fact, probably the most interesting study of parliamentary procedure is connected with the working of parliamentary parties.

The above are some examples, showing the almost infinite variations which are possible within this group of problems. Obviously, continuing along similar lines, we come on a great number of other questions. We will also find that parliamentary procedure can be understood only with sufficient regard to the general constitutional setting, and probably also to the social and functional background. On the other hand, it should not be assumed that it is only a result and not at least to some extent also a cause of general political characteristics. The seating arrangements, the size of the chamber in which parliaments meet, etc., are factors which are not without their importance in influencing the development of political traditions. An interesting example is that of the British House of Commons which has time after time refused to enlarge the chamber sufficiently to provide seating space for all members. Indeed it would probably sometimes be possible to isolate, or at least almost isolate some of these variables, such as seating arrangements, parliamentary procedure, etc. A study of the characteristics of the four parliaments of Denmark, Finland, Norway and Sweden might be interesting in this respect, since the similarities in other respects are so great as to reduce the number of variables.

DEMOCRATIC CONTROL OF FOREIGN POLICY

THE question of by what means foreign policy can be controlled is chiefly a functional one. It has institutional implications, but the main question is that of how a given function, that of control over foreign policy, is actually fulfilled. It is limited in scope and has few interdisciplinary references except in so far as history is concerned. On the other hand, there are a great number of other complications, partly caused by vague and undefined basic concepts.

Democratic control, of course, means control by the people. But how does the people act in matters of this type? It has frequently been assumed that it acts through something called 'public opinion.' But does public opinion really exist, except in the sense of some especially active groups? It may well be asked whether even in the most enlightened countries it can be assumed that the majority of the population have a sufficiently well developed interest in world affairs to exercise real control through the expression of a definite opinion. And even if this is the case there are other complications. It is not always easy to make sure that a certain opinion is really that of the great public and not only of those who are able to cry out loudest. And even if it could be established that a certain opinion is, at a given time, really that of the public as a whole, it might undoubtedly have been falsified through effective propaganda, creating strong feelings on the basis of totally erroneous assumptions of fact. It may be argued that this is one of the general problems of democracy but not particularly connected with the problems of foreign policy; but it is the kind of difficulty which arises as soon as we try to introduce unorganised direct democracy, instead of applying either a referendum or the traditional methods of representation.

Thus, the idea of controlling foreign policy directly by public opinion involves a number of difficulties. But even if reduced to normal representative procedures, it is far from easy. Problems of foreign policy frequently appear at short notice and have not always been discussed in elections. It may be difficult to say to what extent parliament is really representative in this field. This is especially true if we are dealing with narrow majorities, established, perhaps, regardless of party lines. In this case, it may be anything but certain that the majority of parliament is really representative of the majority of the people. Furthermore, a number of external considerations may influence the attitude of parliament. Above all its general political relations to the executive are involved. Parliament may be either willing or unwilling to use its power of control over foreign policy to upset a government when internal policy is the object of heated political controversy along party lines.

But even if we leave these problems aside, accepting, for instance, the idea that democratic control and parliamentary control are the same in the field of foreign policy, we are confronted with a number of problems specific to our field. Any non-governmental control makes foreign policy much more difficult to manage. There are today inter-governmental and supra-national agencies which depend for their work on the ability of the participating ministries and ministers of external affairs of the participating nations to speak for their respective countries and assume liabilities on their behalf. If their action is subject to real control by parliament or some other agency, it becomes very difficult to establish any real results in co-operative organs such as the United Nations. Today—and this is the second consideration—this kind of problem appears not only with regard to the states grouped in the British Commonwealth of nations, but practically everywhere. The manœuvrability of foreign policy is a condition of successful negotiations. Only if the representatives of the countries are able immediately to determine their attitude to new suggestions, ideas and proposals, are they able to wring concessions from the other participants. And, finally, there is the special problem of secrecy. If foreign affairs are 'top secret,' the public, and probably also parliament, will be insufficiently informed of the facts on which they are to base their decisions. If, on the other hand, secrecy is not maintained, the government is not trusted by other governments. The advantages of the 'open diplomacy' were grossly overrated in 1919, and the difficulties of the new system have proved at least as great as those of the old; as explained in the writings of Harold Nicolson.

Some of the direct obstacles in the way of control are, of course, the outcome of these difficulties. Neither public opinion nor parliament have the requisite information and experience to judge foreign affairs. After all, their main interests are elsewhere, and the time they devote to studying international problems is generally very small; whereas these problems are probably more complicated and difficult to judge than the internal problems occupying the major part of the time of parliamentarians. Next, in a number of countries the immediate reactions of the electorate to matters of foreign policy are rather unfavourable. They are 'isolationists', they are apt to take 'a short-range view,' they are 'parochial' in their attitude, etc. Finally, the parliamentary machinery is frequently not suited to this type of question. This may lead to complications or, alternatively, make parliamentary control looser.

An interesting illustration to this was given by Mr. Beloff in a paper to the Florence conference, dealing with the 1947 Berlin conference. It is worth quoting at some length.

'Thus in considering at Berlin the future Germany, the risks of evacuating Germany at all were obviously present to all four Powers. But in the case of the Western Powers the question was one of foreign policy in the ordinary sense: should Germany recover its autonomy, how would it behave, where would it seek alliances, would it be peaceful or once more aggressive? In the case of the Soviet Union, it was more immediate than this. If Eastern Germany were evacuated, its régime could hardly survive; if it were to fall, what would be the repercussions in the other satellites? And could events in the satellites be prevented from calling into question the very foundations of the régime at home? Eisenhower's government does not depend on Adenauer's; but Malenkov may not be able to dissociate himself from the Grotewohl–Ulbricht régime. It is one of the penalties of Communist "infallibility." ...

'This does not mean that Soviet policy is "democratically controlled," of course, in any ordinary sense of the words; it is, however, the product of the same processes as produce all other aspects of the régime's activity, and is not marginal to them. To explore the matter further would be to go outside our proper theme.

'At the opposite extreme to Molotov's position was that of Bidault. As the foreign minister of an uneasy coalition in a country where for understandable reasons it is hard to find a majority to sustain a government on internal matters which is also to be relied upon for united action on foreign policy, Bidault was in a very real sense subject to democratic control. That is to say, his attitude to each question has to be decided upon not simply by what he and his professional advisers may have thought was best for France, but also with reference to the parliamentary situation which in turn was likely to be highly sensitive to public opinion at large. This public opinion itself (unlike Soviet public opinion) lies wide open to influence not merely from various sources at home but also from outside. The weapon of propaganda, which is a relatively blunt one when used against a totalitarian state, is immensely powerful against a divided democracy.

'Foreign critics of France tend to suggest that this situation could be avoided by constitutional changes or even by a simple alteration in the electoral laws. Such criticism is surely superficial. If a régime is strong enough to defy, or itself to mould public opinion on matters of foreign policy, it is unlikely to stop here; but if it went farther, it would cease to be democratic altogether. If it recognises the force of opinion and even of sentiment, then if opinions and sentiments are divided, and if these divisions are passionately maintained, it is hard to see that a change in the machinery is going to alter things very much. If foreign policy is what people are divided about in politics, then you cannot take foreign policy out of politics, unless you can find someone other than the citizens to pay the bills and fight the wars. It is not the number of political parties, at any rate, that matters. In fact, in the French case the divisions within the parties seem as numerous almost as those dividing them from each other.

'One's reasons for taking this view become clearer if we look at the political systems represented at Berlin by Eden and Dulles. Both, it seems, have made some appeal recently to French constitutional reformers.

'The tendencies in British political life towards a two-party system have always been strong, and not simply because the electoral system encourages them. Their primary effect from our point of view has been to make the British system not parliamentary but plebiscitary; that is to say, a House of Commons is created to support, not to choose a government, and for it to withdraw support from such a government means, except in circumstances as unusual as those of 1916 or 1940, the coming into power of the Opposition. Even 1916 and 1940, one might say, led there in the end. Party allegiance is not usually determined by views on foreign policy; foreign policy has in the past been thought of as marginal to Britain's existence, and remained shielded from the public view for a much longer time than any other aspect of government activity; even now the aura of the royal prerogative lingers about it.

'This does not mean that Englishmen always agree about foreign policy. They may even be deeply divided over it. This was the case during the French Revolution, at several junctures in the nineteenth century, and almost constantly during the inter-war period. If the divisions over foreign policy coincide with party divisions, a certain instability may be introduced into British policy; or at least foreign statesmen may believe that this is likely to be the case. Knowledge of this in the past led the British Government to refrain from long-term commitments to action in undefined circumstances. This attitude has failed to survive the impact of two world wars; but its influence lingers inside and outside the country.

'Alternatively, the division may cut across the normal party allegiances in one or even in both parties. This is unlikely to be the case very often. More characteristic is the present situation where the government could probably rely on Labour support against its own rebels over Suez, for instance, while on German rearmament, where Labour is divided, the Conservatives seem at least to be solid. The tendency is, however, for party discipline to work as effectively on matters of foreign policy as on anything else, particularly in the case of a party in power. As a result of this fact, and since on the whole it is the moderates of the two parties who tend to get to the top, British foreign policy appears to present a very considerable element of continuity, despite changes in the complexion of the government like those of 1905, 1945 and 1951.

'It could be argued by those who have been, or are, in opposition to the prevailing trends that this element of continuity marks a derogation from strict democratic control; that neither the ordinary Member of Parliament nor the ordinary citizen has much chance of making his view effective when his action has to be channelled exclusively through the party leaders, who in turn will rely heavily on their expert advisers. It is not very common or fashionable to say this but that is not to say that this is not a situation that could not be proved both to exist in fact, and to be quite defensible in theory.

'It is arguable, as we have noted, that the kind of questions with which foreign policy now confronts democratic governments are incapable of being presented in a form which makes them suitable for discussion or decision by the mass electorates which modern democracy has created, that these are highly technical issues which demand expert handling and that their ventilation in public is likely merely to handicap the country's negotiators. Public opinion cannot be ignored, since it is the public, after all, that must make policy effective; but it must be given a line to follow rather than asked to make decisions for itself. This view involves fidelity to the idea of representation rather than to that of the mandate: you trust your rulers because you believe that their fundamental attitudes are in line with your own and that they can be relied upon in such matters to act as you would have acted if you had their knowledge and experience. It is a position that can only be sustained in a well-integrated national community; but within such a community it can be a major source of strength.

'Nothing could be more different from the British attitude in these matters than the American one. Dulles at Berlin was to some extent in the position of Molotov, and to some extent in the position of Bidault, but there was hardly any resemblance between his role and Eden's. The parallel with Molotov does not carry one very far but, since it is often overlooked, it is worth stating. The United States, like the Soviet Union, but unlike either Britain or France, are to some extent determined in the scope of their policies by devotion to an ideology; they even feel that their internal security is affected by their decisions in the field of foreign policy in a sense which is less true of either Britain or France. The recognition or non-recognition of Communist China is not, for instance, in the ordinary sense a question of foreign policy where the United States are concerned; it cannot be decided without reference to general principles of action and belief. Since America is a democracy, its ideology is much less coherent, much less static and much less all-pervading than the ideology of the Soviet Union, but it cannot simply be disregarded: and although the sanctions against its disregard are less automatic and less painful than those a Russian foreign minister would have to face, they do exist.

'The comparison with Bidault may also seem far-fetched. Unless Dulles loses the confidence of the President (a factor which we can afford to ignore) his tenure of office is safe until after the next election at least, that is to say until January 1957. But although no Congressional majority can get rid of him, Congress can and does demand the right to control him in every detail and possesses in the power to ratify treaties and still more in the power to appropriate funds adequate means for the purpose. He has thus to keep quite as close a watch on the shifts among Congressional groups and personalities as Bidault must do on the National Assembly. Indeed in a sense he is weaker, in that Congress cannot even be forced to try to find an alternative government or policy however far it might go in making his own impossible.

'The Secretary of State, or the President on his behalf, can of course endeavour to compensate for this lack of authority by trying to muster a majority in the country which will bring pressure to bear upon a recalcitrant Congress. All the history of the last forty years goes to show how extremely difficult this is; and the difficulties are rooted in the country's ideology quite as much as in its institutions. Executive government has no general support against the legislature; the idea that foreign policy involves technical considerations which the ordinary citizen is incapable of judging is something unspeakable, almost unthinkable, in an American context. The support for the "Bricker amendment" and other recent evidence goes to show that, if anything, opinion would like to see the executive more, and not less shackled by democratic controls. If the democratic control of foreign policy means letting policy be guided by public opinion, moulded of course by modern mass-media, then the United States give the best example of it of any great Power in the modern world.'

The examples just mentioned show some of the problems in the way of democratic control of foreign policy. They are very real problems and difficult of solution, as opposed, for instance, to the idea that the 'non-democratic' recruitment of the foreign service is a basic factor in determining the development of international policy. The problems of democratic control are created by the character of the functions and the institutions, not by the malevolent unwillingless of some minority groups to accept democratic control.

On the other hand, it is obviously outside the competence of the political scientists to determine to what extent difficulties of this type should make politicians refrain from attempting any direct parliamentary or other democratic control. Their studies will show difficulties in the way; they may, however, also show the way to some solutions. In any case, the comparative approach should be most useful, as illustrated by Mr. Beloff's example. If we compare how the leaders of a nation are placed when consorting with other nations, we get the best possible idea of what democratic control means in practice, how it could be organised, and how its fundamental difficulties might be avoided.

ELECTORAL SYSTEMS AND ELECTIONS

ACTUALLY, a comparative study of elections involves two different problems, closely connected, but yet clearly distinguishable: the structure and functioning of the electoral system, and the actual forces working in elections as expressing the will and action of the electorate. Comparative studies are difficult, both because a number of value judgments are involved, because it is difficult to weigh contributing factors because of the inter-disciplinary problems involved (particularly problems on the border-line between politics and sociology), and with regard to the delimitation of the problem itself. A functional approach, starting from the first question 'How is the opinion of the people expressed?' is almost impossible. We will therefore have to start, at least, with a chiefly institutional approach.

When discussing electoral systems, there is a tendency on the part of most observers to take it for granted that some system (most frequently that of their own country) is definitely superior to all others. This is true especially in countries where democracy seems to be well rooted and has been something of a success for a considerable time. It is natural to an Englishman to assume that majority election in small constituencies is the best method whereas to the Scandinavian some system of proportional representation seems almost indispensable, the only important question being what form of proportional representation should be employed. Those who are conscious of problems in the field of electoral systems frequently see them more in terms of what should be done immediately than in terms of an investigation of what is actually happening. Actually, the same thing applies not only to electoral systems proper but also to the existence and non-existence, respectively, of the referendum. It can be argued that the referendum is part of the electoral system, or at least is similar to electoral systems in being a machinery for ascertaining the will of the people. Here again, those who have it regard it as almost ridiculous to assume that democracy could be wholly representative; whereas nations which have no experience of the referendum rarely show any great enthusiasm over the idea of getting it.

It is not even quite clear whether the question of electoral systems is one of principle or simply one of mechanics. The nineteenth-century illusion of automatic representation seems to be gone. It is difficult today to convince anybody that the will of the people is always there and needs only the proper mechanical device to find its expression. On the contrary, in the light of modern propaganda and of the incredible complication of contemporary political issues, the main problem seems to be whether or not there is a will of the people. Thus, electoral systems are seen not only from the point of view of finding an expression to a popular will which is already there, but rather from the point of view of creating an interest and establishing a will of the people to develop and express their opinions. Alternatively, it is sometimes maintained that the objective is not to give as adequate as possible an expression to the will of the people, but rather to provide some means whereby 'a workable majority' can be established, since it is felt that such a majority can on the whole be expected to pursue a policy acceptable to the people; and this, it is argued, is about as closely as one can ever get to the democratic ideal.

An incredibly great number of systems is actually being practised, from the old fashioned *scrutin de liste* still practised in Turkey, which has the effect of giving even the smallest majority all the seats allotted to a fairly large constituency, to the most refined systems of proportional representation. Only mathematicians are able practically to evaluate the difference between the various systems of proportional representation. A simple basic classification is that proposed by Professor Pollock at the Florence meeting:

(1) Single-member district systems—be they either majority or plurality, with a single ballot or a second ballot.
(2) Proportional representation systems—single transferable vote or list systems.
(3) Other systems—whether based on preferential voting or functional representation or on possible combinations of (1) and (2).

We may, indeed, accept such a classification, although it does not go far enough to help us evaluate the niceties of electoral procedure. For reasons discussed below, these niceties are hardly very important for comparative purposes. The detailed development of a particular procedure may frequently be the result of comparison between procedures used elsewhere in the case of proportional representation. It remains to be proved, however, that there are any particular patterns of development in this field, and so far as we are attempting to relate electoral systems to other aspects of governmental and political structure the main issue seems to be between majority and proportional representation only.

But this applies only to electoral techniques, not to representation as such. There are other specific ideas, such as that of functional, or interest, representation, where the elections take place by special corporations. There are intermediates between proportional representation and single-member district systems, where, for instance, a number of candidates are elected under the one and other candidates under the other system. There are special modifications of proportional representation, such as that employed in Finland to allow voters to influence its elections of persons and not vote only for a party list. There is the system of *apparentement*, that is to say a system allowing for certain priorities between different parties, so that, for instance, the Communist can make sure that his vote, if not helping a Communist candidate, will at least help a Socialist rather than a Liberal or a Conservative. There are what might be called discriminating systems, such as those employed in France and Italy, which favour or rather discriminate against certain parties or types of parties. They may either see to it that very small parties are not given a chance under the system of proportional representation, or make it possible for other groups to form a 'front' against a particular party. These are only some examples of the many different devices employed in the field of electoral systems; the list could be made much longer and in particular much more detailed even without going into mathematics.

Again, we must ask ourselves what is the objective of a particular electoral system. It is impossible to devise any system which gives 'automatic representation' to the will of the people, or indeed gets beyond the great difficulty that a voting body, including the electorate, is hardly able to say much more than 'Aye' or 'No.' Generally, it is not sufficient to say 'Aye' or 'No,' since political life is so complicated. It is sometimes maintained that an election should give a 'mirror of opinions.' But in the first place, the mirror is not very clear; in the second place, it is apt to distort the opinions before it; and in the third place, the picture shown to us in the mirror is influencing us while we pose before it—that is to say the probability of a certain outcome of an election will influence voting, for instance in the case of people refraining from voting for a party which is regarded as being without a chance.

We may also ask ourselves whether electoral systems are really as important as we are apt to believe. Changes in the system may not always be followed by an expected change in results; this has been shown, for instance, by the experiences of Switzerland and of the Third Republic. Parties and candidates, as well as electors, are surprisingly agile in adjusting themselves to different systems; and the result of an apparently fundamental change may well be comparatively insignificant. In any case, the electoral system bears a mutual relationship to the party structure. It is influenced by the latter since, for instance, proportional representation becomes important only in so far as several parties are involved. It also influences the party structure since, for instance, the system of single-member district constituencies makes it difficult to maintain smaller parties in existence, as shown by the experience of Liberals in Great Britain. The importance and the effect of the electoral system depend largely on the historical tradition, and it should be noted that it is frequently much more difficult to alter the party system than to change the electoral procedure. This has been discussed particularly with regard to proportional representation. It has been argued, for instance, that stabilising traits in the constitution, such as monarchy, a referendum, etc., are necessary if a system of proportional representation should work without leading to political instability; and that this is the reason why the system has been applied with more success in Scandinavia and Switzerland than in France and Germany. The argument seems far-fetched. It would be more reasonable to assume that a tendency to stability in the political life of the country leads both to the maintenance of systems such as those of a monarchy and of a referendum and to a party system under which proportional representation avoids most of the dangers appearing elsewhere.

The study of elections themselves, rather than of electoral systems, goes much deeper. It should be seen in relationship to public opinion measurement, for which other methods than elections are also being employed, to group sociology, etc. Always provided that the elections are really free, there are undoubtedly a great number of factors which influence the voting of citizens, and it is not easy to determine which of those factors are most important. The comparison between the result of elections and of referendums is frequently elucidating in this respect. We are also apt to find that citizens do not vote entirely as individuals, but under the influence of social, religious and other groups, each of which have more or less definite political proclivities. It should also be possible to investigate the voting habit of particular groups of citizens. This has already been done with regard to women, and was made possible by keeping, in some cases, a separate record of the voting of men and of women respectively. However, there are other less certain but still quite acceptable methods whereby it can be studied how constituencies with a given social, religious or other structure are apt to vote. Only comparative studies can give an idea of the implications.

There are various approaches to the problem. We may record who is voting at all and who refrains from voting. We may investigate how candidates are selected, who is a candidate, and who is apt to be a successful candidate. We may even determine to some extent *how* groups are voting. We frequently find that there is a regional continuity in the voting habit, both inside a given country (a province or group of provinces, or group of states in the United States is apt to cast its vote in a given direction) but also as between similar areas of different countries. Such comparisons may take place, let us say, between the Scandinavian countries, between the frontier districts of Belgium and France, etc. The need for *comparative* election studies is obvious; on the other hand, the great difficulty lies in even approaching an isolation of variables, particularly where there is a large floating vote.

POLITICAL PARTIES

THE study of political parties is a typical example of a major investigation involving all the particular difficulties appearing in the study of comparative government. There is an obvious need for depth, there is a risk of misunderstanding the situation in unfamiliar environments, and there is a need for an inter-disciplinary approach. Also, we are approaching the question whether or not political facts are unique. On the one hand, the development of political parties is largely based on the historical accidents or the specific cultural pattern of a given country, on the other hand party ideologies are frequently international in character. Practically every study of an important problem in political science leads us back to the party system, and a com-parative approach is indispensable if we are to understand the meaning of parties in government.

It should always be remembered that the essence of a party is its purpose. The objectives of parties appear very clearly in what is generally called a 'competitive' political society, that is to say one where there is diversity of opinions and interests and where it is held to be desirable to allow different opinions and interests to compete with one another. The growing activity of the state, particularly in the economic field, is apt to make not only the state itself, but also the parties competing within it, almost all-embracing: they are required to hold and state definite opinions on practically all matters of human life. But parties themselves are frequently the result of a long develop-ment and party differences are not always adapted to the situa-tion of modern society. Thus, the importance of party differ-ences, and in particular their character, is frequently understood only on the basis of a study of their genesis.

In other cases, such as on the one hand eighteenth-century Great Britain, on the other certain under-developed countries, parties in the sense of the Western democracies exist only on paper. Actually, what we have is a series of 'connections' where the cohesive factor if not so much ideology or interest, but rather the allegiance to a leader or group of leaders. In some cases, clan groups (*hamula*) appear within the parties or sometimes even in the form of parties.

It was argued by one of the participants in the Florence conference that there should be a definite difference between the attitude of the historian and that of the political scientist in approaching the problems of political parties. The former, it was said, should be concerned with the 'origin, development and ideological and institutional factors' of the party system; while the student of comparative politics should ask himself: 'What are the conditions for the existence of the party system?' It is submitted that such a distinction is manifestly impossible, since the conditions for the existence of a given party system are largely historical in character, and especially so when seen from the viewpoint of purposes and objectives.

Most of us would probably be willing to accept the pluralist assumption stated by Professor Macpherson in Florence: 'Since the most important interests of individuals are those which they share with varied and shifting combinations of other individuals, none of which combinations would naturally produce a stable numerical majority, it is clearly necessary, for democratic government, that individuals be brought together in stable grouping capable of sustaining governments. The party system does perform the entrepreneurial function of bringing people together in such stable grouping.' This would to some extent also give an answer to the question: what is the attraction of political parties? But in actual fact, parties are rarely as clearly defined as one should expect on that assumption. On one hand, the class nature of society finds a certain amount of expression in the party system, but on the other

hand political 'bosses,' those who provide the war chests of
political parties, and the parliamentarians who represent them
are frequently influencing the working of parties to a considerable extent. Also, the idea of an 'institutional equilibrium' ✓
seems to be very attractive in theory; but in fact it is not always
easy to see where such an equilibrium has actually been
established.

Over the past two thousand years of party warfare in the
West, many theories and explanations of the party system have
been brought forward and it is indeed not for any lack of trying
that we do not have an accepted general theory of political
parties. But the contribution of comparative government in
this field is probably to be found less in the development of
such theory than in sorting out and mastering a great number
of facts. The inductive approach is indispensable and we should
not be deterred by the fact that it is also the most difficult
approach. What can be done here is no more than to present, as
usual, some of the questions to which we must seek an answer if
our comparative studies of political parties are to be useful.

It may be convenient to begin with studying the legal framework in which parties are working. As a rule, the most important part of this framework is the electoral system, which in
practically all democratic states provides for the existence of
parties or at least tacitly assumes that parties are active in elections. But there may be legal rules for other purposes. Most
countries have some legislation against subversive activities
by organised groups, which by implication may be related to
the political parties and in any case have definite consequences
for the party system. In other cases, 'subversive' parties are
expressly legislated against. Other legal rules may exist to
guarantee equality of chances to the different political parties.
Sometimes the internal structure, including finance, financial
contributions, etc., is the object of legislation. Where the
nominating procedure for elections is regulated in law, this
also influences the structure and working of parties.

In studying political parties, many authors start from the idea of the party 'system.' Their assumption is that democratic government can work only through political parties, and that the objective of studying the party structure is to establish whether or not it is useful for the proper functioning of democracy. In his paper for the Florence conference, Professor Macpherson presented certain hypotheses with regard to the party system:

(a) The main function of the party system is to moderate and contain a conflict of class interests.

(b) The main function of all party systems so far has been to moderate and contain that conflict so as to maintain a capitalist economy.

(c) Nothing except a party system can preserve the stability of a capitalist society where there is popular franchise; or, conversely:

(d) The party system is essential to the maintenance of democracy in a capitalist society.

(e) Whether a two-party or a multi-party system will best serve the purpose of democracy depends on the degree of class stratification and the degree of class consciousness. The more stratified the society, the more easily a multi-party system can be established. The greater the class consciousness, the more necessary a multi-party system is to preserve stability.

Obviously, these ideas apply only in a democratic system of government. In totalitarian society, the most frequent arrangement is the 'one-party system,' which can be left out here, since it is really a negation of the idea of political parties.

General observations on 'party systems' deal chiefly with two alternatives: that of a two-party system and that of a multi-party system. Actually, however, these two ideas are not altogether clear and there is also a twilight zone between them.

As an example of the two-party system, the United Kingdom is probably most often quoted. But as a matter of fact it has only been for comparatively brief periods that a real two-party system has existed in England. The idea is, therefore, sometimes modified to include what has been called the 'two and a half party system,' that is a system where the emphasis lies on two traditional parties but where minor groups operate, as it were, between or beside the major parties and sometimes, although not as a rule, may hold the balance between them. The habitual example of the 'multi-party system,' on the other hand, is France. But it should be remembered that during many periods the party system in France has been so complicated that it has been difficult to establish conformity within each of the many existing parties. The French system is, therefore, very different from that applied, for instance, in the Weimar Republic where the number of parties was considerable but each of them presented a united front to the others. There are other modifications of the multi-party system. One of them is what has been called the 'bi-polar multi-party system,' for example as applied in Western Germany today where there are two powerful groups, the SPD and CDU, and in addition a number of smaller parties operating with the major groups but unable to assume power on their own. In fact, this situation is very similar to what was called in the case of England the 'two and a half party system.' Another example is that found during certain periods in the Scandinavian states, where one party (generally Labour) has held a bare majority or almost a majority over all other parties, whereas the different groups of the opposition have operated separately and sometimes shown greater or smaller willingness to co-operate with the major group.

It can be argued that party systems are in a sense 'unique' to each particular country. On the other hand, there are striking similarities, and it should be remembered that a number of political parties are based on ideologies which are more or less international. This, of course, is particularly true of Labour groups, but it applies to an increasing extent to other parties also.

Thus, political parties can as a rule be studied only genetically. The essence of parties lies in their objectives, and a study of party 'systems' therefore seems to be comparatively useless unless related to the actual forces expressed in existing parties. The 'systems' may change with the purpose involved (for instance in Western Germany, in the Scandinavian states, etc.) and on the whole the party structure is influenced less by the idea of being useful to Western democracy than with regard to the actual interests expressed. Historically, parties mostly originated in the work of parliament, not in extra-parliamentary forces. There are exceptions to this rule, the most important of which is the growth of Labour Parties in a number of countries. But on the whole, parties were formed first as groups of parliamentarians and only at a later stage organised to gain the necessary popular support for their views. The classical example is Great Britain, but the same applies to most other countries having a long party history behind them. In studying political parties today we have to take into primary consideration the relationship between the national organisation on the one hand and the parliamentary representatives on the other. The role of professional politicians, whether inside or outside parliament, comes into the picture more or less at the same point.

The study of political parties, therefore, should necessarily include, although it need not necessarily begin with, a study of the parliamentary groups, their working procedure and their relationship to other authorities such as the cabinet, the committees, etc. It should go on to investigate relations between the parliamentary party and the national organisations: the influence of the latter on parliamentary work and the influence of parliamentary groups at election time. It must also include the question of the governing 'inner circle' of the parties, which may be the same in and outside parliament but may also show differences and even conflicts between parliamentary and extra-parliamentary leadership. Finally, there is the fundamental question of leadership itself. A student of party activities must pay considerable attention to the technique of parliamentary leadership, as well as to the techniques of extra-parliamentary leadership and electoral propaganda. In this connection, case studies could be very useful, and they should probably take the form of studies of the working of particular political leaders, such as Lloyd George and Churchill in England, Clemenceau in France, the two Roosevelts, Dewey and Eisenhower in the United States, etc.

The role of political parties in democracy includes many other problems. In some countries, it is necessary to study the position of political parties with regard to the use of the referendum. Switzerland should be a particularly good object of such studies, but a number of the states of the United States should also be included; a comparison should be very interesting. On the other hand, the parliamentary work of parties includes also questions such as that of coalition in parliament, whether temporary or permanent, and the effect of a parliamentary coalition on the extra-parliamentary work of the party.

In studying the extra-parliamentary organisation of the party, the focus of interest is held by the question of membership. Membership of the party is frequently, or even invariably, strikingly different from its voting strength and may even not be directly related to the latter. One party may have considerable voting strength and yet a low membership, whereas another group is putting more emphasis on organising its voters. In particular, it is important to study which voters become members—if it is limited to those who are more or less directly active in the party, those who are giving it financial support, etc. From the point of view of the nominating procedure, we should also investigate to what extent membership gives particular influence over the nomination of candidates, so that those who support the party without being members have to abide by the nominations decided upon by active members.

Another type of question is related to the organisation and procedure of national, district and local party bodies. In this case, there are considerable differences between countries, but also between types of parties. Labour Parties are a particularly interesting study in this respect and the difference between Social Democratic and Communist Labour should also be considered. However, the bourgeois groups also have a number of interesting characteristics. A question related both to membership and to organisation and procedure is that of collective membership, especially of the Labour Parties, where in a number of countries the labour unions are directly affiliated.

Parties appear, of course, as a rule most intensely at election time. A study of the nominating procedure, including presidential conventions in the United States, legally regulated primaries, etc., should be included. But we must also deal with the propaganda apparatus. What is the part played in election propaganda by the party machine as compared to that of candidates themselves? And finally, there is the question of coalitions between parties in elections, which is closely related to that of the electoral system, but also gives expression to the types of relationship existing between political parties in general and some of them in particular.

But the fundamental questions are those related to the basis of parties. It is here that we find the core of the problem. The idea of 'party systems' is related to the individualist assumption that every individual citizen has his own political opinions, which he is trying to express in some sort of combination with others. Burke's definition of a party starts from this assumption which again should be seen in the light of the idea of some sort of 'automatic' representation of opinions through an electoral system. In our day, it is more and more generally assumed that the individualist assumption is, in fact, not correct, and that citizens are seeking the expression of group interests rather than of individual opinions. This has also led to a situation where political parties are consciously or unconsciously seeking the support of powerful economic groups, and where not only their practical policies but even their basic ideologies are influenced by these attempts.

This implies a modification of the Marxist interpretation of political life as a struggle between classes. In its modified form, this interpretation is today almost a commonplace. No one would deny that there is a close relationship between class and party and in particular between economic interest and party affiliation. Indeed, ideas of this type appeared long before Marx and may be said in a certain sense to form the basis even of Rousseau's idea of the general will, or, as it should perhaps have been interpreted, the general interest. Not that Rousseau is accepting their idea that political life is a struggle between different interests, but he is, as it were, contradicting this idea on the assumption that there is an interest—and therefore a will —which is general in the sense that it represents all different interests. At this point, comparative studies are indispensable. The class nature of society differs from one country to another and it is partly because of these differences in the class structure that the party system also has developed along different lines, for instance, in Western Europe and in North America.

On the other hand, even a modified Marxist interpretation has its limitations. Not all parties are socially homogeneous. Some of them, such as the Labour groups, have a least a definite basic class content, but others consist of supporters with very different social backgrounds. Also, cultural patterns are frequently just as important as economic interest. There are parties based on religion or nationality. A Marxist might possibly argue that it is only on the surface that parties are based on such ideologies as these, and that the latter are themselves the result of a social structure, being used to gain support for interests which are totally different from those of the people who actually support the parties. But this interpretation is today very rarely accepted outside extreme Marxist circles. As a rule, it is admitted that ideologies do have a strong force over human beings, and recent developments in Western Europe seem to have strengthened this assumption. In any case, a comparative study of parties of this type should go a long way to show what is the real importance of the ideology as compared to economic interests.

Another difference between parties and party systems is related to their attitude to one another and the aims which they are pursuing. Some parties are 'militant' in the sense of seeking the realisation of their aims almost regardless of the consequences and of their relationship to other groups, whereas others are more tolerant, relativistic and co-operative. These differences are related to the background and the purposes of the parties, but also to the general social and political atmosphere of the country.

Another important factor is how the policy of the party is actually determined—by groups of voters, by parliamentary representatives, by 'bosses' or by those who provide capital for the party. This brings us to the working relationship of parties to interest groups. Whatever the organisational relationship, there is always the possibility of a conflict of allegiances, a possibility which, incidentally, exists in the case of different interest groups also. A voter who is a member of a given political party or habitually supports it at elections may find that the policy of the party does not coincide with the policy of an interest group of which he is also a member, just as he may find that membership of two different interest groups leads him into an equivocal position. Thus the study of political parties should be completed by comparable studies of interest groups, whether 'pressure' or other groups. Such studies become particularly important where there is direct co-ordination of political parties and interest groups.

Finally, it is necessary to study parties not only from the

point of view of their political activities, but also as 'social movements.' In this case, in particular, they must be compared with other popular movements. For it is undoubtedly true that in a number of cases party activities play and, perhaps, particularly have played a very important part in the general social life of the community. This fact also has considerable influence on the position which a given party may have at election time: those who look to the party to give them desirable social contacts are also willing to give it their political support.

It appears that the approaches to a study of party systems and political parties are almost innumerable. A number of different methods must be applied simultaneously, and one of the most important is that which has been labelled 'microsociology.' Studies of party activities in smaller units—both during and between elections—should probably go a long way towards explaining the general character of the party system in a given country. At least in so far as detailed statistics are available, this presents the political scientists with a fertile and wide field of study, not only of each country by itself, but also for purposes of comparison.

CONTEMPORARY REVOLUTIONARY
MOVEMENTS AND REVOLUTIONS

THE study of revolutionary movements and revolutions again involves a difficult combination of problems. The concepts themselves are very vague in both cases. The approach must largely be interdisciplinary. Yet the questions themselves are fundamental to the study of politics, especially if we should go beyond the traditional study of Western democracies where revolutions are at present not part of the normal political procedure. Outside the West they are more frequent and most elucidating.

There are two reasons for the vagueness of the concepts. In the first place, the definitions are anything but clear. We shall come back to this question later, but it should already be mentioned here that the very term revolution is used in many different senses. And, secondly, whatever the sense in which we employ the term it is strongly loaded with value content. This fact also makes it much more difficult to attain any generally accepted definitions of the term.

Also, the interdisciplinary aspects are probably more strongly marked in this case than in any of those we have been discussing so far. Revolution is perhaps not even principally, and in any case not entirely, a problem of politics. On the other hand the political importance of revolutionary tendencies is unlimited. We cannot study the political aspect of revolutions without going very far into economic, social and cultural factors. But on the other hand, it is also impossible to study the politics of a country where revolutionary tendencies appear without taking them strongly into account.

The term 'contemporary,' as used in this context, is also

rather difficult. What is 'contemporary?' And why should our studies be limited to the circumstances of today? It is true that there are certain traits which appear more definitely after the Second World War than before, such as the fact that isolated revolutions seem to be more or less unlikely and that there is an ideological 'cold war' which may lead to revolutionary movements. But otherwise the traditional type of problem appears now as before. A comparative study of revolutions and revolutionary movements could, for instance, never leave the French revolution of 1789 or the Russian of 1917 out of the picture. More recent experiences have to be related to these 'classical' examples, if for no other reason than because they have so thoroughly influenced the ideology of revolutions in general.

Another general introductory remark seems to be in order. The interest of men, whether seen as individuals or as collections of more or less organised groups, is almost invariably pragmatic. We are interested in results and willing to accept procedures to attain those results. This is the fact which frequently stands in the way of the maintenance of the established order, whether that order be democratic or not. It is hardly true to say that revolutions are even generally caused by attempts on the part of the people, or important groups of the people, to attain more influence in the abstract. What they want is to improve their status, not in the abstract, but with certain very concrete objectives. Where the established order seems to fulfil their objectives, it is rather easily maintained. Where this is not the case, revolutionary movements may take place even in order to substitute dictatorship for democracy.

Any study of revolutions and revolutionary movements must, therefore, begin by an attempt to clarify definitions. We must know what we are talking about, even if only in the form of presenting a number of equally valid alternatives and determining which of them to choose.

The term 'revolution' itself is, as has already been pointed out, frequently used in different contexts. It is sometimes applied to signify any sweeping change, in whatever field and by whatever means. Sometimes the idea of suddenness and swiftness is included: a revolution is a change which takes place in a short time; but this idea is a very relative one, and the shortness of the period may be related to the magnitude of the change. Others are willing to employ the term 'revolution' only in the case of changes which involve the use of violence. Also, opinions vary very much as to how deep and far-going the change should be to justify the term revolution. We may, for instance, draw a distinction between a *coup d'état* and a revolution, on the assumption that the former is a change only in the top stratum of government, whereas revolutionary changes are those which upset society as a whole. We are confronted by these difficulties in many fields, and one of the most well-known examples is that of the 'industrial revolution' which in Western Europe took place over a period of almost a hundred years and was certainly not fundamentally associated with the use of physical violence. On the other hand, the term is so generally accepted that it is difficult to employ any definition of a revolution which leaves the idea of the industrial revolution out altogether.

The value-loaded attitudes to revolution also vary. A revolution is sometimes seen as an undesirable interruption of normal development; sometimes as desirable interruption of a development which is regarded as undesirable. Sometimes it is seen as a normal, periodically recurring means of change; and there are also a number of ideologies according to which 'the Revolution' is a permanent state of affairs. It should be noted that these value-loaded distinctions are not parallel to those of the preceding paragraph, but that on the other hand they frequently influence the choice of terminology.

Another value-loaded concept is that of the 'counter-revolution.' This, again, is not very clear. It may be employed to signify a change bringing about the re-establishment of an order existing before the revolution. But it may also be used for any activity which is opposed to the revolution as a permanent state of affairs or at least to the full development of its aims and objectives.

The semantic difficulties recur when we are discussing revolutionary movements. Obviously, the definition depends on how we understand the idea of revolution. A revolutionary movement may be one advocating sweeping change in general, one advocating sweeping change to take place suddenly, one attempting to use violence to effect such a change, or simply one planning to seize power by means of force. Here again, we have to make it clear what we mean. Also, we have to make it clear whether we are dealing with movements advocating sweeping change by political means only or also with those which regard political aspects as of subordinate importance compared to the social changes at which they are aiming.

What has just been said shows the difficulties appearing in the field of definitions. It is not attempted in this connection to fix any definite definitions. The necessity for defining terminology should be obvious in any case; and it is particularly important in comparative studies, since we find that there are differences in concept, and also in value attitudes not only between different authors and different ideologies, but also between different countries. What is regarded as revolutionary in one country is regarded as a perfectly normal development in another.

Passing from terminology to substance, we find that the number of question marks is no smaller. If we are dealing especially with the present situation, we may find, as has been stated already, that isolated revolutions seem comparatively unlikely. The element of foreign influence in revolutionary movements seems to be stronger at the present juncture than it has been at any time since the beginning of the nineteenth century. And this is important, not only to the study of revolutions themselves, but perhaps particularly to the study of the revolutionary movements. It has important practical consequences. The possibility of using a *coup d'état* as an instrument of revolution—even if the *coup d'état* is not itself regarded as revolution—is particularly great under such circumstances. And we are also confronted with what has been called the managed revolution—'*Revolution von oben.*' A government, originally established by perfectly normal and even democratic means, may use its position to liberate itself from constitutional shackles and effect far-going and deep changes in the social and political structure far beyond what was envisaged at the time when the government was established. On the whole, in circumstances such as these both the spontaneity of revolutions and their social and ideological bases are particularly difficult to evaluate.

In fact, it may prove useful to limit the problem and to concern ourselves at least chiefly with spontaneous and independent revolutions. In this case, we have to study on the one hand the contents and on the other the dynamics of revolutions.

When, speaking of content, we are apt to think chiefly of social or class content. This does not necessarily mean 'working class' content. The dynamic factor in a revolution need not be the working class at all, but may be any group which is sufficiently strong to carry out revolutionary changes. On the other hand, not all social conflicts lead to revolutions. One of the questions we have to ask is, therefore, why the social forces are seeking a revolutionary instead of an evolutionary expression. Where, for instance, is the point at which the social group despairs of attaining its objectives within the existing social and constitutional framework and takes matters into its own hands? When confronted with far-going demands for widened political power for the working classes, Guizot answered: '*Enrichissez-vous, Messieurs.*' The answer was generally regarded as ridiculous, and it became a catchword of the revolution. But what Guizot meant was probably that the groups in question would in the long run gain their objectives by normal economic development, if they were only willing to wait. In Great Britain, they were willing to do so at the time; in France they were not. What was the explanation? Similar problems appear in many other countries and at many different times.

But we must also remember that social forces in the sense of economic and related interests are not the only cause of revolutions. History knows many examples where, for instance, religious groups have resorted to revolutionary means, and it would be an over-simplification to assume that, for instance, Fascist movements in Western Europe were entirely the result of economic conflict. Also there is the question of the relationship of revolutionary movements to totalitarianism. It is true that revolutionary movements frequently are unconscious of the totalitarian aspect of their objectives, but it is equally true that the cause of revolutions is sometimes found in the fact that only a total—and therefore at least temporarily totalitarian—revolution brings about the social and ideological effect desired by the revolutionaries.

The dynamics of revolutions require equal consideration. It is far from certain that revolution needs either active or even passive support from the majority or even from a really large group of the population in order to be successful. History shows that intensity of feeling has frequently proved a sufficient substitute for numbers, and Leninist ideology has given us a considered argument in support of this observation. Revolutions frequently are made possible by what is generally called a 'spark,' putting fire to combustible material. But it is equally true that careful preparation has, and particularly so in modern society, proved a very important factor for the success of revolutionary attempts. Also, there is the trite observation that revolution continues, as it were, by its own force and that revolutionaries themselves find it very difficult to stop at the point where they originally attempted to do so. One of the points where we need further research—and where historical comparison could prove useful—is *why* this has proved so difficult.

Closely connected with the study of revolutions is the problem of by what means the established order is able to defend itself effectively against revolutions. In order to find an answer, it is necessary to study not only successful revolutions but also those which have been unsuccessful. And in particular we have to investigate what is, in a given environment and at a given time, the primary attraction for support of revolutionary attempts.

When studying revolutionary movements which have as yet not succeeded in their attempts, we are, of course, confronted with the usual problems of definitions. Practically all strong political movements are revolutionary in the sense that they aim at far-going changes of the political and social structure. On the other hand those who are in favour of the established order are frequently apt to regard practically all movements aiming at such changes as revolutionary, or alternatively as counter-revolutionary. Here again we have to be wary of accepting the terminology which is being used in the countries which we are studying.

The attitude of revolutionary movements to totalitarianism is another object of study. In order to be valid, such studies should investigate the character of the movement both before and after a successful revolution, and perhaps particularly during the 'revolutionary period' itself. We are here also meeting the famous dilemma of Liberalism, that is, whether revolutionary movements should be permitted to use the freedom which they are not going to grant to others once they have been successful. Also, the element of foreign pressure comes into the picture. Especially at the present period, revolutionary movements are frequently basing their activities largely on support from the outside.

Another question is that of the structure of revolutionary

movements. To what extent are they dominated by small groups, largely drawn from the intelligentsia? And to what extent do they find it necessary to gain really widespread support?

Finally, the existence of revolutionary movements which are completely reckless in their propaganda influence the normal activities of other political forces as well. It frequently leads to what has been called an 'auction' involving all groups in propaganda where they promise far more than they can actually achieve. Such a situation has the additional effect of creating general unrest and dissatisfaction, and whether revolutionary movements are conscious of it or not, it definitely favours their aims by establishing what might be called a 'revolutionary situation.' This is true of a number of countries today and should be an important factor in our studies of political parties. Thus, the question of revolutionary movements is closely tied up with the problems discussed in the preceding section. On the other hand the timidity of 'normal' parties may be one of the causes of recklessness on the part of other movements and an explanation of their revolutionary character; a fact which provides important material for the study of the political situation as a whole.

INDEX